a girl's gotta do what a girl's gotta do

THE ULTIMATE GUIDE TO LIVING SAFE & SMART

KATHLEEN BATY
"THE SAFETY CHICK"

RODALE

Notice

This book is intended as a reference volume only, not as a self-defense manual. The information given here is designed to help you make informed decisions about your personal safety. It is not intended as a substitute for formal training of any kind. If you suspect that you have been a victim of a crime, we urge you to contact your local police department.

Mention of specific companies, organizations, or authorities in this book does not imply endorsement by the publisher, nor does mention of specific companies, organizations, or authorities in the book imply that they endorse the book.

Addresses, Web sites, and telephone numbers given in this book were accurate at the time the book went to press.

Book design by Christopher Rhoads
Interior photographs by Mitch Mandel/Rodale Images

Library of Congress Cataloging-in-Publication Data

Baty, Kathleen.
    A girl's gotta do what a girl's gotta do : the ultimate guide to living safe and smart / Kathleen Baty ; foreword by Gavin de Becker.
        p.   cm.
Includes index.
    ISBN 1–57954–639–0 paperback
    1. Women—Life skills guides. 2. Women—Crimes against—Prevention.
3. Crime prevention. 4. Self-defense for women. I. Title.
HQ1221 .B285 2003
646.7'0082—dc21   2002014994

Distributed to the book trade by St. Martin's Press

2 4 6 8 10 9 7 5 3 1   paperback

Visit us on the Web at www.rodalestore.com, or call us toll-free at (800) 848-4735.

Dedication

This book is dedicated to U.S. Congressman Ed Royce, who is committed to his constituents and not notoriety. Ed is an intelligent, moral man who took a stand on stalking before any other politician, man or woman, would do so. For that, all us Chicks should be grateful.

I also owe Ed a personal debt of gratitude for believing that I could make a difference before I believed it myself.

Contents

Acknowledgments

I want to thank the following people for helping me evolve into the Safety Chick:

My husband, for always being behind me 100 percent (except when I go shopping).

My three wonderful boys, for being the coolest dudes I could ever have hoped for.

My father, the true writer in the family and my personal editor, who showed incredible restraint by not changing my "slang" writing style into proper English.

My mother, for standing over my father's shoulder and not letting him rewrite the manuscript.

My brothers, Kevin and Rob, for making me tough when I was a little girl by pinning me down and pretending to spit on me but kindly sucking it back into their mouths before it hit my face.

My law enforcement friends John Lane, Dr. Chris Mohandie, Rhonda Saunders, and Greg Boles, all of whom I respect immensely and with whom I have greatly enjoyed working as their civilian sidekick.

My Keystone buddy, for showing me that working with law enforcement is fun!

Ron Brooks and Tom Elfmont, for taking care of business.

Andy Cohen, for "getting it."

T-Bone, for being my stylist, interior decorator, and all around best chick.

Jodi Campbell, for being the definition of strength and courage.

Kate White, for "planting the seed."

My agent, Bonnie Solow (and Jessica!), for believing in the mission of the Safety Chick.

Stephanie Tade and all of the great, down-to-earth people at Rodale.

Chris Potash, my editor, who puts up with all my bad jokes and is now a hip Safety Dude!

I'd also like to thank a number of experts who graciously contributed their professional know-how to better this book: Matt Thomas, Chief Bill Fenniman, Vali Hashemian, Gavin de Becker, Paxton Quigley, Francisco Guerra, Dave Nielsen, John Flowers, Sergeant Marc Dowdy, and Sergeant Deborah Bazan. These people are top authorities in their fields, and I respect them deeply for their dedication, passion, and hard work.

Foreword

by Gavin de Becker

Every creature on earth has a defense system. In the beginning of a girl's life, parents are the defense system, designed to spot danger at the earliest possible moment and well qualified to avoid it, evade it, or destroy it. Then there comes a day when the people initially responsible for her safety welcome a new member to the team: the girl herself. Seemingly overnight, the eyes that used to casually take in the sights will have to detect danger, assess it, deter it, perhaps even confront it.

Imagine a young woman about to make this transition. If Kathleen Baty is not her teacher, I wonder who will be, for few parents really know how to prepare their daughters for a safe journey through life.

Every girl and every woman who reads this book will learn to honor her feelings; if someone makes her uncomfortable, she'll know that's an important signal. She'll learn that it's okay to rebuff and defy anyone, that it's okay to be assertive. She'll learn that it's okay to strike, even to injure, someone whom she believes poses a danger to her. She'll learn that if a predator says "Don't yell," the thing to do *is* yell. That's because when someone says "Don't yell," he is actually saying that yelling would serve you and silence would serve him. Too many people feel compelled to cooperate in their own victimization, in part because they assume they'll be hurt if they don't.

Every reader can learn from Kathleen to fully resist ever being taken anywhere out of public view by someone she does not trust, and in particular by someone who tries to persuade her. A predator who orders you to go somewhere with him is really telling you that he wants to take you to a place where he'll be able to do whatever it is he can't do here. It is essential to re-member that initial injury is far from the worst consequence of a violent crime.

Kathleen and I both encourage women to explicitly rebuff un-wanted approaches; we also know that this is difficult to do. Ex-plicitness applied by women is highly unpopular in our patriarchy. A woman is expected, first and foremost, to respond to every communication from a man, and her response is ex-pected to be one of attentiveness. In the context of approaches from male strangers, however, warmth only lengthens the en-counter, raises his expectations, increases his investment, and, at best, wastes time. At worst, a woman's uncertainty can serve the man who has sinister intent.

When I encounter people hung up on the seeming rudeness of responding explicitly, and there are many, I imagine this conver-sation after a stranger is told no by a woman he has approached:

MAN: "What a bitch! I was just trying to offer a little help. What are you so paranoid about?"

WOMAN: "You're right. I mean, just because a man makes an unsolicited approach in an underground parking lot in a society where three out of four women will suffer a violent crime; and just because I have to consider where I park, where I walk, whom I talk to, and whom I date in the context of whether someone will kill me or rape me or scare me half to death; and just because these are life-and-death issues most men know nothing about so that I'm made to feel foolish for being cautious even though I live at the center of a swirl of possible hazards— *that doesn't mean a woman should be wary of a stranger who ignores the word 'no.'"*

Though many men can't relate to this, the truth remains that women, particularly in big cities, live with a constant wariness. Their lives are literally on the line in ways that men just don't experience. Ask some man you know, "When is the last time you were concerned or afraid that another person would harm you?" Many men cannot recall an incident within years. Ask a woman the same question and most will give you a recent example or say, "Last night," "Today," or even, "Every day."

Still, women's concerns about safety are frequently the subject of critical comments from the men in their lives. One woman told me of constant ridicule and sarcasm from her boyfriend whenever she discussed safety. He called her precautions silly and asked, "How can you live like that?" To which she replied, "How could I not?"

Kathleen and I have a message for women who feel forced to defend their safety concerns: Tell Mister I-Know-Everything-About-Danger that your survival instinct is a gift from Nature. Tell him that Nature knows a lot more about your safety than he does. And tell him that Nature does not require his approval.

Many women believe that violence is a mystery that can be understood only by men, but Kathleen knows better. Throughout this book she shows that intuition is deep, brilliant, and powerful. Nature's greatest accomplishment, the human brain, is remarkable enough day in and day out, but when its host is at risk, it moves to a whole new level, one we can justifiably call miraculous.

The brain that protects each woman was field-tested for millions of years in the wild. I call it the *wild brain*, in contrast with the logic brain so many people revere. The logic brain is burdened with judgment, slow to accept reality, and spends valuable energy thinking about how things ought to be, used to be, or

could be. The logic brain has strict boundaries and laws it wants
to obey, but the wild brain obeys nothing, conforms to nothing,
answers to nobody, will do whatever it takes. In fact, the wild
brain doesn't give a damn what we *think*.

To tap into this resource, to reinvest in intuition, you must
listen to internal warnings while they are still whispers. The voice
that knows all about how to protect you may not always be the
loudest, but it is the wisest—and Kathleen speaks in that voice as
she teaches lessons from her remarkable perspective. She has been
tested more than once, and she has established herself as a powerful woman with stunning survival resources. More important,
she insists that you are just as powerful, regardless of your size,
your age, or your perception of your own physical abilities.

When I first read *A Girl's Gotta Do What a Girl's Gotta Do*,
I knew that it could help the one audience most difficult to reach:
teenage and college-age girls. With the information in these
pages, they will be able start their adult lives from a position of
power. Sadly, that's not the norm, for young women are the most
victimized segment of our population. At the same time, they are
the least likely to report a crime.

In a survey of prison inmates who had committed violence,
three quarters of their victims were girls. Why? For starters, they
offer less resistance and pose less risk than other victims. Further,
predators are able to exploit the fact that teenage girls are themselves exploring the dynamics of male attention. Many girls see
fearlessness as a form of sophistication, and this is the time when
they are first away from parental supervision, take a first job,
have a first date, first experiment with drugs and alcohol.

All these factors combine by the time a girl has reached her
teens, when she has gone from being an occasional sexual predatory prize to the leading sexual predatory prize. Accordingly, I don't
think there's information about personal safety that a woman of
any age needs to be protected from. Her understanding of how per-

suasion strategies work and her understanding of how targets are selected is her armor.

Women educated by Kathleen will be more likely to see the signals that I saw on a flight from Chicago to Los Angeles. I was seated next to a teenage girl who was traveling alone. A man in his forties who'd been watching her from across the aisle took off his headphones and said to her, with partylike flair, "These things just don't get *loud* enough for me!" He then put his hand out toward her and said, "I'm Billy." Though it may not be immediately apparent, his statement was actually a question, and the young girl responded with exactly the information Billy was hoping for: She told him her full name. Then she put out her hand, which he held a little too long.

In the conversation that ensued, he didn't directly ask for any information, but he certainly got lots of it. He said, "I hate landing in a city and not knowing if anybody is meeting me." The girl answered this question by saying that she didn't know how she was getting from the airport to the house where she was staying. Billy asked another question: "Friends can really let you down sometimes." The young girl responded by explaining, "The people I'm staying with"—thus, not family—"are expecting me on a later flight."

Billy said, "I love the independence of arriving in a city when nobody knows I'm coming." This was the virtual opposite of what he'd said a moment before about hating to arrive and not be met. He added, "But you're probably not that independent." She quickly volunteered that she'd been traveling on her own since she was thirteen.

"You sound like a woman I know from Europe, more like a woman than a teenager," he said as he handed her his drink, a Scotch, which the flight attendant had just served him. "You sound like you play by your own rules." At first, she declined to take the drink, but he persisted. "Come on, you can do whatever you want," he prodded, and she took a sip of his drink.

I looked over at Billy, looked at his muscular build, at the old tattoo showing on the top of his wrist, at his cheap jewelry. I noted that he was drinking alcohol on this morning flight and had no carry-on bag. I looked at his new cowboy boots, new denim pants, and leather jacket. I knew intuitively that he'd recently been in jail. He responded to my knowing look assertively. "How you doin' this morning, pal? Gettin' out of Chicago?" I nodded.

As Billy got up to go to the bathroom, he put one more piece of bait in his trap: Leaning close to the girl, he gave a slow smile and said, "Your eyes are *awesome*."

In a period of just a few minutes, I had watched Billy use several of the predatory strategies I've studied during my career. Most significantly, I'd seen him discount the girl's *no* when she declined the drink; that is always a reliable indicator that someone is trying to control you.

As Billy walked away down the aisle, I asked the girl if I could talk to her for a moment, and she hesitantly said yes. It speaks to the power of predatory strategies that she was willing to talk to Billy but a bit wary of the passenger, me, who asked permission to speak with her. "He is going to offer you a ride from the airport," I told her, "and he's not a good guy."

I saw Billy again at baggage claim as he approached the girl. Though I couldn't hear them, the gist of their conversation was apparent. She was shaking her head and saying no, and he wasn't accepting it. She held firm, and he finally walked off with an angry gesture—not the "nice" guy he'd been up till then.

There was no movie on that flight, but Billy had put on a classic performance of predatory persuasion, one that, by little more than context—forty-year-old stranger and teenage girl, alone—I could tell was a high-stakes matter.

I wish I could have handed that teenage girl a copy of this book. With several now in my briefcase, that's exactly what I'll do next time.

So . . . Who Is This "Safety Chick"?

In November of 1982, I answered a phone call that would change my life forever. A former high school acquaintance decided to fixate on me and make my life a living hell. The first incident involved harassment and a brief arrest by police for threatening phone calls. In the years that followed, his threatening behavior escalated and finally culminated with an attempted kidnapping and an 11-hour police standoff. The stalker had finally committed a felony. There were no laws on the books declaring stalking a felony, and every time this person violated a restraining order, the penalty was just a brief stay in county jail. This time, he was convicted of attempted kidnapping and served four years in prison. Over the years I gained first-hand knowledge of how our legal system works, and trial-by-fire skills that saved my life. But first I had to learn how to deal with the many emotions that victims experience during this kind of ordeal.

I started out in denial. After the first incident of harrassing phone calls, I said to myself, "Well, that was sure strange, but it will never happen again." I was a junior at UCLA, and went back to school, thinking it was over. The second incident occurred three months later when he showed up at my parents house with a gun in his pocket looking for me. (I was out.) He was arrested by police a few hours later across town, and held on a 72-hour psychiatric hold. On the advice of the police, I obtained a restraining order. I said to myself, "Why me?" and spent a lot of time wallowing in self-pity. I remember thinking, "Why didn't he pick the Homecoming Queen?" and "What did I ever do to him?"

"What does not kill me makes me stronger."
—Johann Wolfgang von Goethe

Three years passed before he struck again. I injured myself jumping over a wall as he was trying to enter my apartment. He was arrested for violating the restraining order and I ended up with stitches in my leg. At that point, I abandoned my career, moved home, and began living like a victim. Every life choice I made related to my personal safety. I put my dreams on the back burner and did what I thought was "safe."

In 1990, I married Greg, who was a tight end for the Miami Dolphins. Friends would say to me, "Don't you feel safe with your six-foot-six, 250-pound husband at your side?" I responded, "Unfortunately, brawn is no match for bullets." The stalker was never deterred by any male in my life, regardless of size. The night Greg and I returned from our honeymoon, I got a courtesy call from the local police saying that the stalker had been released from jail after serving four months for violating a restraining order that I had put in place. Not quite the wedding gift I had in mind.

The next week Greg left for training camp in Miami, so once again I had to fend for myself. One afternoon, I came home from work and was listening to my answering machine. When I turned around, the stalker was standing behind me with a knife. I had to make a choice. Was I going to be a victim or a survivor? Was I going to give up and let fear overtake me, or was I going to fight and use my head? That "little voice inside" that you will hear me talk so much about in the following pages was yelling loud and clear: "Calm down, get control of the situation, and get the hell out of here!"

To be honest with you, I was a little relieved. For so many years the police kept saying to me, "Until he lays a hand on you, there's nothing we can do." So my first thought was, "Thank God, we've finally got a felony!" The first words that came out of my mouth were, "Sit down, I've been expecting you. . . . We need to talk." As it turns out, those were powerful words. He thought that I would become hysterical—like every horror movie he'd ever seen. He was probably hoping I'd faint. All I know is that my calm demeanor and matter-of-fact tone completely threw him. It gave me the psychological edge I needed to maintain control of the situation. It was definitely a greater power that orchestrated the events that followed and got me out of there alive. My determination and the fact that I escaped unharmed were nothing short of miracles. After a bizarre standoff with police in my driveway, he was arrested.

While these events helped shape my life, I did not let them define who I am. In the years following the kidnap attempt, I did a lot of soul searching. I had to deal with all the pent-up emotions—the anger, frustration, and fear—or I was going to explode. I decided that I needed to get my "power" back; I finally was tired of living like a victim.

It was then that a wonderful man named Ed Royce contacted me. He is now a U.S. Congressman, but at that time he was a California state senator. He had written legislation that would make the crime of stalking a felony. Congressman Royce had read about me in the paper and asked if I would testify before a state senate committee as a victim in support of this potential law. Here was my chance to actually put these awful events to good use. As I sat in front of the committee recounting each event, I began to feel a power inside me that I had not felt in a long time—the inner knowledge that I was in control. I no longer had to live like a victim. The way to get my power back was to become proactive. Congressman Royce and I teamed up again in Washington to help pass the first federal antistalking legislation, which President Clinton signed into law in 1996.

"My best feature would have to be my resilience."
—Michelle Pfeiffer

Over the years I have testified in front of several legislative committees, been the keynote speaker at law enforcement seminars, appeared on dozens of television shows, have been the focus of documentaries and police training videos, and helped write a stalking telecourse for police officers. I've been the subject of hundreds of newspaper and magazine articles. Most meaningful to me has been working with law enforcement officials all over the country. Their commitment to public safety amazes me. I have had the opportunity to learn priceless lessons from some of the greatest experts in the field.

I have been an athlete all my life, so training with a former Navy SEAL and learning self-defense techniques from a French mercenary who fought in the Lebanese army was awesome. I started to realize that this personal safety thing was not only empowering, it was fun! I started writing a column called *Streets Smarts with Kathleen Baty* for a security Web site that sold personal safety products. I appeared on television shows as a personal safety expert. I showed viewers how to use pepper spray, stun guns, and other safety items. I tried to present the information in a way that was informative yet entertaining. People started to refer to me as "The Safety Chick," and the name stuck.

A couple of years ago I decided that I really wanted my hard-won knowledge to count for something. I decided that I would write a book. But I did not want to write my life story; I didn't want to be seen as another one of those made-for-TV movie victims played by a has-been movie star, or the token victim interviewed on local news after the movie. I knew that all women would be better served by practical safety tips and the benefit of my extensive research and personal insight. If I could prevent one woman from becoming a crime victim, that would be worth it.

"If you want to be in films, wait tables— don't get kidnapped."
—Patty Hearst

The result is the book that you hold in your hands. May it increase your peace and bring you empowerment.

Go Chicks!

Introduction

Safety Savvy

Why It's Hip to Be an Empowered Chick

Some women don't care about crime prevention. They believe that thieves don't see them, that thugs can't touch them, that stalkers wouldn't stalk *them*, and that victims live only in big cities or on the other side of town. Some of these same women brag to me that their neighborhoods are so safe that they rarely lock their doors.

I'm here to tell you that you don't need to be a crime victim to care about your personal safety. In fact, that's the whole point: I don't want you to become one. I learned about personal safety the hard way. My goal is for you to live your life with confidence and common sense so that you'll never be ambushed by crime like I was. Believe me, we can all increase our level of personal safety. You just have to choose to do it.

The information in this book took me years to acquire and sort out. I don't expect you to read it over a weekend and immediately apply every safety tip. Think about what security concerns you have now, and go from there. I do expect that some issues will strike a chord with you; others might strike a chord with your mother, daughter, girlfriends, neighbors, or co-workers. Don't be afraid to talk about personal safety. You will be surprised at the response you get from other women. Someone always has a story to tell of how they or a close friend was touched by crime. With the great safety tips you'll learn from this book, your gal pals will soon be coming to you for advice and affectionately calling *you* the Safety Chick.

In my experience I've found that pamphlets on crime prevention generally take the tone of a lecture (read: boring), while the scenarios imagined in many books on personal safety are so terrifying that important information gets lost in the gruesome tales. No girl needs that. Acquiring safety savvy should be a positive experience, one that empowers, not scares you. And so in my book I offer an arsenal of personal safety solutions delivered in a clear, concise, and intentionally lively style. My intent is to hold your attention while alerting you to serious situations in which you may someday find yourself—and clueing you in on how to get out of trouble or, better yet, how to avoid it in the first place.

As you get into the book, the surprising number of professionally proven defense strategies may seem a bit overwhelming. You might even think that following all these tips and guidelines could mark you as . . . well, unhip. But I promise you that the effect will be just the opposite: Using the tools in this book will eliminate that uncomfortable feeling of being vulnerable in strange situations. (There's a time and place to feel vulnerable, girl, and it isn't when you're being threatened by a stranger.) Living as a Safety Chick means living bold, self-assured, and smart.

The book begins by introducing the key to personal safety: your intuition. Whether you prefer to think of it as your inner voice, your radar, your antennae, or simple common sense, intuition is a powerful natural security system that's always on duty—all you have to do is tune in to its constant signals. The rest of the chapters address specific security issues of particular concern to women. Three or four main Safety Chick tips are provided for each predicament to help you recognize when you might be in danger and to propose detailed, easy-to-implement solutions.

"Common Sense is not so common."
—Voltaire

I've learned first-hand how to protect myself in all of these situations, and so throughout, for the sake of the sisterhood, I'm happy to share with you the stupid and risky things I've done over the years to put myself in harm's way. I'll also share some funny and not-so-funny anecdotes that show just how practical this safety stuff can be.

At some point you may notice that I repeat certain ideas; this is not by accident. Common sense is a lost art, and it bears repeating to sink in. The Safety Chick Checklists at the end of the chapters are provided for your convenience and can be referenced whenever you're packing for a business trip, preparing for a quiet night alone, or when you need to act quickly, such as when your credit card has been lost or lifted, you've just been assaulted, or you're being harassed at work or home. At the very end of the book you'll find a list of federal agencies, trade associations, watchdog groups, and private companies that will provide additional information and personalized help for all of the safety issues raised in this book.

Finally, while acknowledging that some women might feel

awkward being called a Chick, I want to assure you that this Chick considers it—and delivers it—as the highest compliment. To me the title suggests a modern woman who's sure of herself, yet fully feminine. Forget all those horror movies where at the first sign of danger the girl screams, turns to run, and inevitably breaks her high heel. Safety Chicks are way too savvy for that! With the information in this book, any woman can feel confident and comfortable in almost any situation, even while wearing a fabulous pair of Manolo Blahnik stilettos.

Women of the world, unite! It's time for us all to become personally empowered Safety Chicks. As you read and learn, remember our motto: A girl's gotta do what a girl's gotta do!

Chapter 1

Intuition

An Absolute "Must Have"
in Your Personal Safety Wardrobe

When I was in college, I had a chartreuse Volkswagen Bug convertible. It was so bright, it glowed. The car radio had been stolen for the fifth time, and I hadn't replaced it yet, so the only way I could listen to music was with a Walkman. So there I was, Miss Thing, driving in a questionable part of LA with the car top down, headphones on, and UCLA cheerleading pom-poms in my back seat (not too much of an airhead), completely oblivious to what was going on around me. Thank God a policeman had the good sense to pull me over and give me a ticket. (It is against the law in California to drive with headphones on.) He was not amused by my girlish charm, and rightfully so. After giving me a much-needed scolding, he sent me on my way. As he drove away, you could almost read his mind: "When are these girls going to learn?"

You hear it time and time again: Listen to your gut instinct, or *intuition*. Fact is, it works. If you just take the time to get in tune with your surroundings, nine times out of ten you will be able to avoid a negative situation before it happens. If only we'd done that with many of our ex-boyfriends.

We are all going a hundred miles an hour from sunup to sundown. We barely take the time to eat lunch, let alone get in touch with our inner selves. This is a big mistake. To live safe and smart, you *must* use your intuition. It's like that little black dress—without it, your wardrobe is not complete. You cannot even begin to tap into your intuition, however, if you are preoccupied.

"The only real valuable thing is intuition."
—Albert Einstein

Crime victim after crime victim will tell you that their attacker caught them by surprise, or that they didn't know what hit them. Taking the time to be aware of your surroundings can save your life. I cannot impress upon you enough that it is *not* about feeling paranoid, it is about being street smart.

Intuition just means acknowledging what you already know inside. Recognizing that butterfly feeling in your stomach or the prickly sensation down the back of your neck means that your inner self is trying to tell you something. It could be "Something isn't right," or "This guy is really a putz." Learning to sense your body's intuitive signals is the first step to personal safety. Without intuition, all the safety tips in the world won't help you.

One of the most compelling books about the value of intuition is *The Gift of Fear*. Written by Gavin de Becker, a leading expert on threat assessment and violent behavior, this book was an early benchmark in the campaign to alert women to the lifesaving need to listen to their intuition.

As he studied dozens of cases and interviewed scores of victims and near-victims, De Becker was able to uncover the consistent presence of intuitive thought among women in dangerous circumstances. Those who recognized and acted on their feelings often emerged unscathed. Those who ignored it frequently were not so fortunate.

To help you identify how intuition works among your own range of reactions, I've come up with a couple of examples I'm sure you will recognize. Think about each, and apply them to your daily life. If you find these scenarios all too familiar, you need to change your behavior. Get in tune with your intuition. Who knows? It might even improve your love life!

Come In, Tokyo!

How to tune in while driving around town

Have you ever gone to the grocery store and been so preoccupied thinking about what you needed to buy that when you pulled into the parking lot, you couldn't remember driving there? That's what I mean by not being aware of your surroundings. Save the daydreaming for when you're sitting at home, sipping wine in front of the fireplace. When you are out on the street, you need to have your antenna up and working. Driving teachers will tell you not to have your radio so loud that you can't hear the siren of an emergency vehicle. The same is true for potential carjackers or robbers: If you can't hear them coming up beside you, when you finally notice them, it may be too late.

The Window Washer and Other Strangers Who Approach Your Vehicle

Has a stranger ever attempted to wash your windshield or ask for money while you're stopped at a light? Did you flinch as the stranger approached your car? If so, that was your intuition telling you to be careful. Don't ignore those signals! While I am a huge believer in charity, donating at the street corner is not safe. Keep your window rolled up and don't make eye contact. Save the contribution for a local cause or shelter.

You Are Not AAA

If you come across a fellow motorist broken down alongside the road, your best course of action is to use your cell phone to alert the police and let them handle it. If you don't have a cell phone, note the car's make, license plate, and location, and call the police when you get to your destination. Your first impulse might be to pull over and try to help, but common sense should tell you that the days of helping strangers by the side of the road are over. It doesn't mean that you can't be helpful and compassionate; it just means that you have to be those things in different ways.

Get Off My Tail

Have you ever been driving and noticed that the same car has been behind you for several blocks? What made you notice? Did something inside prompt you to look in your rearview mirror? Once again, that's your intuition wondering, "Hey, wait a minute, is someone following me?" Don't ignore the signal. If you think a car is following you, make a turn and then another. If the car is still behind you, call 911 on your cell phone and drive straight to the nearest police station. (There aren't too many criminals brazen enough to commit a crime in a police station parking lot.) If you do not know where the police station is, drive to a really busy area and find a brightly lit gas station. Do *not* lead a criminal to your house, where he can follow you up your driveway.

Shiver Me Timbers

When the little hairs on the back of your neck stand up, pay attention

Close your eyes, take a deep breath, and relax. Don't worry, I'm not going "New Age" on you—I just want you to listen to your heart beating and your lungs breathing. Your body does these miraculous things somatically (automatically), without your noticing. The goal is to respond to your body's signals quickly without thinking about them.

Beach Blanket Bingo

You're on the beach, walking down to the water in your cute little bikini. (Okay, maybe your support one-piece.) You automatically suck in your stomach—that's your intuition, or "gut" instinct, telling you that some hunk on a towel next to you might be checking you out. How about when you're walking down the street and the little hairs on the back of your neck stand up? That's intuition, too. Don't ignore that feeling. If you are too busy being scared, you won't think clearly. Take the time to glance behind you and around you. Do you see someone or something that is out of place, a possible cause for concern? If you do, listen to your no-nonsense inner voice that says, "Okay, calm down and don't panic." Is there a store close by that you can go into? Is there a group of people you can stand near? (Preferably not a group of gang members.) The key is to quickly assess the situation so you can remove yourself from harm's way.

The Chilly Willies

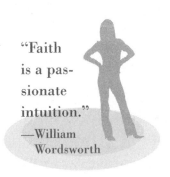

"Faith is a passionate intuition."
—William Wordsworth

A chill down the back of your spine is another indication that your intuition is working. If you're jogging on the street or on a trail and you feel the chill, don't ignore it. Don't be embarrassed to turn around and look to see if someone is sneaking up behind you. Confront the situation. It might be just your neighbor out walking his dog, but it could be someone intending to do you harm.

If you exercise outdoors, try to do so with a friend. If you must exercise alone, there are all kinds of great little safety products to take along with you. (Check out the Resource Guide at the end of the book.)

Butterflies Are Free

Butterflies in your stomach can signal a number of things, but they are an intuitive signal nonetheless. Whether you are about to make a presentation in the board room or take a test in the classroom, your body is signaling you that you are nervous or excited. But another reason for the butterflies might be more serious. The distinction is a subtle one: The butterflies might be more of a tightening in your stomach. For example, if you enter a party or nightclub and feel that the energy of the crowd is tense or hostile, then your intuition is telling you that something bad could happen. A fight could break out, or worse. Listen to the signal and get out before anything happens.

These are just a few of the common body signals that you might recognize. Think about your reactions in such situations. Test yourself the next time you're driving to the market or out walking. Identify situations in your daily routine that would require you to use your intuition.

If Looks Could Kill

You *can* judge a book by its cover

When you meet someone in a public setting—a bar or health club, for example—have you ever thought, "This person is a little strange"—and not just because he's wearing a polyester leisure suit? That is your inner voice saying, "Steer clear." Women have been conditioned to be polite to everyone, including some obnoxious men who won't take no for an answer. Don't worry about being called a bitch. Don't worry about being rude or hurting someone's feelings. Many rape victims wish that they had not been so nice to that stranger at the bar.

The Eyes Have It

There are many ways to sense if someone is a possible danger to you. A good indication is by looking into their eyes. You know the saying: The eyes are the window to the soul. Well, if a person's eyes appear glassy or glazed over, chances are this is not someone you want to be around. Another signal is if the stranger stares at you inappropriately. There is an acceptable amount of time that a stranger should look at you. *You* decide that amount of time. Once you start to feel uneasy or self-conscious, the stranger should look away. Continued staring should alert your intuition.

Space Invaders

Do you feel uncomfortable giving a perfect stranger private information? A department store clerk, perhaps, wanting to know your social security number. That's your intuition asking, "Now, why would she need to know that?" Many victims of credit card fraud are shocked to find that the criminal was the person at the local store. Be aware of people standing around you when you are giving out personal information. There is such a thing as needing your space, especially when a con artist is trying to learn your address, telephone number, and social security number.

When someone is standing too close behind you, ask yourself a couple of questions. Are you two the only ones at the counter? If so, why is the person standing so close? Is the person paying inappropriate attention to your transaction? This is not to imply that every nosy person is a criminal; if that were true, all of our mothers-in-law would be in jail. It's just that you need to be aware of the people around you, and if something doesn't feel right, do something about it. Remove yourself from the situation.

What's That Smell?

Many rape victims have reported that their attackers had a specific aroma, and I'm not talking about a lack of deodorant. According to Matt Thomas, author of *Defend Yourself: Every Woman's Guide to Safeguarding Her Life*, many rape victims report a strong ammonia-like scent that seems to emanate from people who are charged up on adrenaline and possibly ready to attack. That smell should act as a warning signal for women. Think of scent as another tool in assessing whether a stranger is dangerous.

The Memory Game

Signs that alert you if something is amiss

Your house or apartment is the perfect place to play the memory game. Putting common household objects in strategic places is a good way to detect burglaries or break-ins. By remembering the exact position of a flowerpot on a windowsill, you would easily be able to tell if someone had disturbed it. Or lean a box or package against your front or back door, and if it has been moved or knocked over, take it as a sign that something is amiss. These simple exercises can help back up and sharpen your intuition.

Did You Remember to Take Out the Trash?

Have you pulled into your driveway and thought, "Funny, I don't remember leaving the garbage can there?" or "I thought I left that outside light on when I left this morning." As you drive into your driveway or walk up to your door, notice if the windows are the way you left them. Are the screens on? Are windows that were closed when you left now open, or worse—broken? Use your memory to help keep you safe. If you feel that someone is there, or has been there, don't go inside. Go to a neighbor's house or stay in your car and dial 911. The police are more than happy to check things out for you. They would rather have one crime (burglary) to investigate than two (assault or worse).

Later in the book I will go into detail about what to do after your intuition has signaled your body to act, but first I want you to get a feel for what intuition is and how it works. Identify your own inner body signals. Practice the exercises I talked about and take the time to make them second nature. Once you take responsibility for your own safety, you turn the fear of becoming a victim into empowerment.

Chapter 2

Girl on the Go

Travel and Hotel Safety Tips
for Women on the Road

I once appeared on a television talk show called Carol and Marilyn *in an episode that dealt with women who had been crime victims and had managed to turn their negative ordeals into positive action. One, a mother of two grown boys, traveled regularly for her work. The traumatic trip she described started out like any other. She checked into her hotel after attending business meetings all day. Her room was located on the outside courtyard on the bottom floor. Unfortunately, she was not paying attention when she entered the courtyard. Two thugs snuck in behind her, and when she opened the door to her room, they pushed her inside and raped her for several hours. I was amazed by this woman's resilience and strength. She not only survived the ordeal, but she has made it her mission to lobby for truth-in-sentencing laws for violent felons in her state.*

The story above is not meant to scare you but to teach you a couple of valuable lessons. One: Never stay in a hotel room on the bottom floor; it makes it too easy for criminals to break in. Two: Always be aware of your surroundings.

Maybe you've got a client meeting in New York this week, a company dinner in Los Angeles the next. Sure, it sounds glamorous, but as anyone who travels often on business knows, jet-setting can be exhausting—and potentially dangerous. Pickpockets love large cities with lots of people because it is easy for them to blend in with the crowd as they go about their business of robbing the unprepared and unaware—but definitely *not* a Safety Chick. Transportation is another area that can pose a safety hazard. Taxicabs, subways, even renting a car can be dangerous if you're not paying attention. When you are aware of your surroundings and listening to your intuition, criminals are not likely to rear their ugly heads.

If you are a scuba diver, you know the phrase "Plan your dive, dive your plan." What that means is: Know where you are going and what you are doing: Have a plan. Do not arrive in a city without hotel reservations. Do check the weather; you don't want to be driving around an unfamiliar town in a blizzard. Do get a map of the city and various places that you're going to visit so that you can become familiar with the area before you arrive. Do get on the Internet or call a travel agency or a tourism board to get all the information you need about the places you will be visiting. Don't become another tourist crime statistic: As the Scouts say, "Be prepared." (I was a Camp Fire Girl, and while I never mastered the art of making fire from a couple of twigs, I *know* our chocolate mint sticks could give any Girl Scout cookie a run for the money!) Analyzing the particulars of where you are traveling is the first step in being prepared for safety. Do your research. For example, when traveling overseas, you should contact government agencies like the state department or bureau of consular affairs (see resource guide at end of book) to find out the current political climates of potentially hostile countries. This kind of information not only makes your stay more efficient, it makes it relaxing and enjoyable. It will help you earn your merit badge for safe travel.

Throw Out Your Steamer Trunk

How to pack and travel like a seasoned pro

Unless you have your own personal valet, you need to get rid of bulky bags and downsize. Heavy bags slow you down. If you need a forklift to haul your suitcase through the airport, you've packed too much.

What to Pack

There are so many great clothing lines that have good-looking mix-and-match wardrobes now that you don't have to "pack the farm." Consider sticking with the same color of clothing so you only have to bring one pair of shoes. You know you can never go wrong with black—it goes everywhere and doesn't show stains from the morning-cup-of-coffee spill. Anyway, don't pack your entire closet for a few days of fun. Every woman should be able to pack for a week with just one suitcase—on wheels—and a tote bag. (I will allow you to bring back one *small* bag in addition to your suitcase, particularly if you've been to some fabulous shopping destination.) But in addition to that cute little black dress, there are other important items that every savvy Safety Chick must bring on a trip to ensure her safety.

A flashlight. You never know when the power might go out in your hotel or you need to read a road map. Make sure it has fresh batteries.

Prescription medication. Keep them with you, not in your suitcase. You do not want to become separated from vital medication, especially if you can become incapacitated or ill without it.

A first-aid kit. The basics to include are Band-Aids, aspirin, and antibiotic ointment. You don't want to have to make a drug store run in the middle of the night in a strange city.

A battery-operated alarm clock. You can never totally count on wake-up calls, and if the power goes off in the hotel, you'll want to know how long until daylight.

A prepaid calling card. Somehow, you never seem to have enough change.

A list of emergency contacts. Keep this in the hotel safe along with all your important business and personal documents. In case anything should to happen to you, hotel personnel or the police could contact your family or your doctor.

A copy of your itinerary. Leave this along with your emergency information stored in your purse or briefcase and leave a copy for your family at home. In an emergency, people will know where you are—or where you should be.

A photocopy of your passport. Also, an extra passport picture, no matter how much it looks like a mug shot. If you lose your passport, this can help expedite the replacement process.

A photocopy of your driver's license. Also, a copy of your insurance information and a copy of your credit card numbers. Again, this helps if your wallet gets stolen.

I know this sounds like a lot to do, but trust me, it's not that big of a deal. If you have ever had your wallet stolen or lost your bags, you know what a pain in the you-know-what it can be to replace everything, especially when you're not at home. Many a vacation has been ruined by the loss of a wallet or a passport. By taking these extra steps, you can make sure you're enjoying a cocktail by the pool, not stuck in your hotel room on the phone with the credit card companies or the passport office.

Don't Bring Your Bowling Bag

You also need to carry a sensible purse, one that closes with a secure clasp and can be worn diagonally across your shoulder so that the purse is in front of your body. The cute little backpack is definitely a no-no when traveling. Backpacks are a pickpocket's dream. Great travel purses are the ones that lie flat on your chest and have a wide strap that crosses over your shoulder and around your back. These are tough for robbers to rip or cut off your body. Remember, the more difficult you make it for the criminals, the more likely they will leave you alone. Several department stores carry this type of purse, so it should be easy for you to find.

What Not to Pack

Another groundbreaking invention for women is cubic zirconia. This wonderful man-made stone is definitely a girl's best friend when she's traveling. Save the real diamonds for showing off at home. Traveling with valuables is like taking a spin on the roulette wheel. Do you really want to risk losing your sentimental or expensive keepsakes because you wanted to wear them on a trip? If you must take valuables, be sure to carry them on your person—do not pack them in your suitcase. Your luggage could be lost or stolen. Once you are in your hotel, lock any valuables in the hotel safe. When you are traveling you want to blend in, not stick out like a sore thumb. Save that sassy Victoria's Secret ensemble for the cute date at dinner; wear the classic wardrobe when you're en route to your destination.

It's *Not* the Bags That Make the Man (or Woman)

Having Louis Vuitton luggage might make you feel like a million bucks, but all it really makes you is a target for criminals. The plainer the luggage, the better. Stick with solid colors and attach a luggage tag that you can identify. Speaking of luggage tags, *never* put your full name or address on your luggage tag. Your first initial and last name—M. Smith—is sufficient. Only give a phone number where you can be reached if your luggage is lost, preferably your work or cell phone number.

You and Your Bags—Attached at the Hip

Another problem with traveling with heavy or too many bags is that it makes you appear disorganized—an easy mark. All a thief needs is for you to look away for a split second to make his move. One distraction, and that bag is his. Don't ever take your eyes off your belongings. If you have more than a carry-on, try to check your bags at the curb. The less you have to deal with your luggage, the better. Skycaps are usually very busy and cannot keep an eye on your belongings the whole time. Make sure you wait and watch until your bags are safely inside the terminal and on the conveyer belt.

Beware of the Bait-'n'-Switch

The security checkpoint is where some of the best con artists work. The heightened security since September 11 makes it even easier for cons to steal your belongings. A common ploy is that when you put your bags on the belt, one con steps in front of you, and barges through the metal detector ahead of you. This guy usually sets off the detector, causing further delay. While all this is going on, another con is waiting on the other side for your bag. As it comes through the x-ray machine, he quickly grabs it, and is on his way.

Cameras used to be the favorite pick for the cons, but now it is laptop computers. Whatever the item, make sure you can see your bags at all times. If there is a delay at the metal detector, put your bags on the conveyer belt just before you walk through, so you are there when your bags come off the belt. Never take your eyes off your bags. If you are traveling for an extended period of time and you need more luggage, consider shipping some of your things to your hotel. That way, you not only eliminate any safety problems, you also eliminate the possibility of dealing with the lost luggage department (a.k.a. The Black Hole).

Traveling should be a relaxing and fun experience, and it can be when you take the time to be prepared. Following these common-sense packing tips not only makes your travel easier, it makes you one prepared Safety Chick! Your den mother would be so proud!

Now that you've arrived safely, you need to get to your hotel or other destination, which brings me to my next tip.

Taxi!

Cabs, subways, rental cars: How to get from Point A to Point B safely

Planning ahead can be a real lifesaver—literally. You should arrange for a car or limousine service to pick you up at the arrival terminal. If you don't already have the name of a car service in your destination city, call the hotel where you will be staying and ask them for a recommendation. That way, you know that your transportation has been arranged and the company is legitimate. It also saves the time and hassle of hailing a cab or finding some other form of transportation at a crowded terminal. Some hotels have their own buses or minivans. Find out ahead of time where to meet your shuttle and how often it runs. If you're arriving late at night, you don't want to be waiting for your ride. By arranging in advance for a driver to pick you up, you have the comfort and safety of knowing that someone will be waiting for you.

Taxis

Taxicabs are among the easiest and safest ways to get around in a big city. Aside from their sometimes scary driving habits, cabbies can be quite entertaining and informative. But like anything else, a few bad apples (or fraudulent cab drivers) can spoil the batch. Make sure you are in a legitimate taxi. Don't fall for the driver who conveniently has a little "free time" and would gladly give you a ride to your hotel. Many con men wait for tourists at airports and train stations, hoping to nab a few unsuspecting travelers and take them to the cleaners when it comes time to collect the fare.

Large cities regulate the number of taxis on the street. Legitimate taxis must have a medallion—a registered cab company license. Airport information desks or taxi stands are the best places to get a cab. Be sure to ask them what the current metered rate is for taxis, so that you have a rough idea what your fare will be. Don't forget to use your intuition to sense if the meter is running too fast and you are getting ripped off. Always ask the cab driver what his metered rate is *before* you get in the cab.

Money, Money, Money

Taxi companies have strict mandates that they must follow and are monitored periodically by the city. All medallion companies must charge the same metered rate in that city. It is usually around $1.50 to $2.00 to get into the cab, about $1.50 per mile and a wait time of anywhere from $10 to $40 an hour which kicks in if, for example, you ask your cabbie to wait for you while you're shopping or having dinner. Find out the "wait rate" before you go inside and have a leisurely meal.

Let's Make a Deal

In some foreign countries, however, there are *no* regulations. Anyone who owns a car can be a taxi driver—this makes it a dog-eat-dog business, which can be dangerous for visitors. Foreign taxi drivers love tourists because they consider them easy money. All fares are negotiable, so be sure to ask your driver what the fare will be and come to an agreement *before* you step in the cab. Again, it's also a good idea to have the hotel arrange a car service, so you know it is a reputable company. Ask the concierge or desk clerk what the going fares are, so you can be a little more informed *before* the foreign cabbie takes you for a ride.

Sprechen Sie Deutsch?

It is very helpful to learn a few key phrases in the language of the country you are visiting. "How much are those adorable shoes?" is a good start, but more important examples are "Where is the bathroom?" and "How much is the taxi fare to the restaurant?"

Safety Chick Taxi Tips

If a cab is your transportation of choice, be sure to follow these Safety Tips when traveling here or abroad:

1. **Always use an established taxicab company.**
2. **Ask what the rate is before you get into the cab.**
3. **Do not share a cab with someone you do not know.**
4. **Do not share personal information with the cab driver.** Keep the topic of conversation on the weather or local places of interest. *Use your intuition.* If you're uncomfortable, or if something isn't right with the driver, get out of the cab.
5. **Always make a note of the cab number and driver's name and license number.** This is important information to have in case the cabbie does something stupid, or worse. Also, words cannot describe the feeling of watching your wallet drive away into a sea of yellow taxis. This info can help you get it back.
6. **Make sure that the meter reads "Zero" when you start your trip.** If not, politely ask your driver to reset the meter.

7. **Tell the driver you would like him to take the most direct route.** (If you're in the mood for a little sightseeing, arrange for a bona fide tour.) Ideally, you should plot your path on a city map ahead of time so you know where the driver should be taking you.

8. **Put a business card or matchbook of your hotel in your purse before you leave so you can be assured that you will return to the right place.** Do you know how many "Hyatts" there are in New York City?

9. **If you are out at a restaurant or nightclub, ask the host or hostess to call a cab for you, and be discreet about giving out your name and where you are staying.** You do not want to be hailing a cab in the middle of the street late at night.

10. **If you've called a cab, wait for the driver to come in and ask the host or hostess for you.** Make sure he is from the company that was called. Fraudulent drivers sometimes wait around restaurants or bars to pick up unsuspecting patrons.

11. **Do not get out of a cab in a dark, desolate, or poorly lit area.** Make sure the driver drops you off right in front of your destination.

Subways or Trains

When you are using the subway or train station, try really hard *not* to look like a tourist—and I don't just mean not wearing your dark socks with your shorts and sandals. Standing in the middle of a subway station staring at a large map of the city makes you a beacon for cruising criminals. Plan your day and destinations before you leave your hotel. Have the concierge or front desk clerk help you out with directions and train schedules. If you have questions once you're in the station, ask the clerk selling the tickets or tokens. (You may also ask the clerk for a subway map or train schedule to look over back at your room.) Once again, keep an eye on those personal belongings. Subways and train stations are usually very crowded; purses are stolen in the blink of an eye and the thief easily disappears into the crowd.

Go to the Light

Don't ever get into an empty subway car. Remember: safety in numbers. If you find yourself in an empty car, simply exit at the next stop and switch to a crowded one. (Do *not* walk between cars while the train is moving.) The best place to sit on a subway is in the front middle of the train. Look for a blue light on the top of the car. This is usually where the conductor stands and regulates the comings and goings of the passengers. If any problems arise, he is the first person to call security. Finally, pay attention to where you are so you don't miss your stop.

Subway Car Etiquette

Riding on the subway is quite a unique experience. While it's fun to do a character study of the people who ride, it's best not to make eye contact. In some countries eye contact can mean a whole lot more to a man than, "My gosh, that's cheap cologne you're wearing." Watch yourself—many women have been groped on train and subway cars. Some men will take any opportunity to cop a feel. If this happens to you, make a loud objection, complete with hand gestures. In any language, the point gets across.

The Recap

The key is to be inconspicuous. Don't wear flashy clothes or jewelry, don't show your money or travelers checks in public, and keep hold of your personal belongings. Don't forget to grab on to a pole or seat as the car takes off; there is nothing more embarrassing than falling face down in the middle of a subway car.

Rental Cars

Renting a car can be quite a frustrating experience. You'd think that car rental agencies love to test your patience by having long lines with only a handful of agents working. Then, when it finally is your turn, somehow they have no record of your reservation. Sometimes you're lucky, and your name appears on their computer screen. That's when you're told they are out of cars for the moment and would you mind waiting for a few hours until one becomes available? Recently I traveled to Los Angeles on business, and the rental car company didn't have the car that I had reserved. In order not to be late for my meeting I agreed to drive a very large Ford F-150 pickup truck. Try parallel parking that sucker in LA! Regardless, don't let the frustration of the rental process make you unaware of your surroundings.

Back Off, Bucko

Many criminals wait around car rental lobbies to eavesdrop on your personal information, such as credit card or driver's license numbers. Remember to be aware of people standing around you. Fill out your rental forms on your own—don't shout out your personal information to the agent. Hand them your credit card and driver's license and let them punch the information into the computer.

Night Moves

Don't ever rent a car at night. There usually are only one or two employees on staff, and getting to your car in a dark parking lot isn't safe. It's also difficult to get your bearings when driving in an unfamiliar town in the dark. If you get in late, take a cab or car service to your hotel and rent your car in the morning.

Baby, You Can Drive My Car

Have the rental car agent show you exactly where your car is. You don't want to be wandering around the parking lot, looking for your slot number. Once you have reached your car, get in, lock your doors, and take your time familiarizing yourself with all the knobs and switches. Do you know how to turn on the lights? How about the windshield wipers? My husband was caught by surprise when we were on vacation in Florida. It started raining hard—really hard—and he couldn't find the windshield wipers. He almost took out a whole line of palm trees.

Check the gas tank: Is it full? Which side of the car is the gas cap on? Adjust your seat and all the mirrors before you put your car in drive. These are important details to note *before* you pull out of the parking lot. You don't want to be stranded on the side of the road out of gas in a strange city. Once you've picked a jamming radio station—not *too* loud, you want to be aware of your surroundings—you're ready to hit the road. Do you know where you are going? Do you have a map and detailed directions to your hotel or other destination? Don't forget to have change for tolls you might encounter on the way.

Charting Your Course

Not to keep harping on the Scout theme, but now is the time to be prepared. You definitely don't want to be driving around a strange city without knowing exactly where you are going—I mean down to every left- and right-hand turn. In some areas of the city of Miami, one block can be a beautiful section of million-dollar homes and literally a block later is a neighborhood of crack houses and crime. One wrong turn could mean trouble—you definitely need to know exactly where you are going. If you are not sure of the directions, ask the car rental agent to chart it for you on a map. If you are still not clear, call the hotel and talk to the concierge or someone at the front desk.

Details, Details

Be sure to write down the make, model, color, and license plate number of your vehicle; it usually is on your key chain, but if you lose it or something happens to the car, you will need that information for the rental company. Don't advertise that you are a tourist. Leave all maps and brochures of tourist traps like the local wax museum in the glove compartment, and make sure your luggage and valuables are locked in the trunk. Remember that the purpose of any kind of transportation is to get to your destination safely.

Checking In?

Essential safety measures for women arriving, registering, and staying at a hotel

When I am traveling alone on business, one of my favorite parts of the trip is staying in the hotel. It gives me time to unwind: no kids wanting me to get them juice or find their baseball glove; no husband wanting to know what's for dinner—just peace and quiet. But in order to completely relax, I always follow these safety guidelines when I stay anywhere, and so should you.

Arriving

First, if you have a rental car, make sure to pull right up to the front to check in. If there is a bellman on duty, he will help you with all your bags. If possible, valet park the car. If your hotel does not have a bellman or valet service, pull up to the front to check in and leave your car there while you unload your bags, but do not leave your keys in the car, and lock your doors. Go register, get your bags to your room, and then park your car. Make sure you park close to the front entrance and in a well-lit area.

Again, be aware of your surroundings. Is anyone lurking around the parking lot? If so, don't get out of your car. Instead, drive to the front of the hotel and get one of the employees to escort you to and from your car.

Hotel, Motel, Holiday Inn

If you are staying at a motel, your company needs a bigger budget (ba-dum-bum). Seriously, a motel poses bigger safety issues than a larger hotel. Usually your room is right next to cars parked in the lot, which allows criminals to watch you come and go. Never park in a space that is the same as your room number. Explain to the desk manager that for safety reasons you wish to park in either an unmarked space or one with a different number. Any person could watch you leave your space and break into your room while you're away; or worse, wait for you to return.

Security Blanket—A Room Next to the Office

Another problem with a motel is that it usually doesn't have the security measures of a hotel. Most hotels have security guards on duty at all times; motels usually only have the front desk clerk. Any problems would be dealt with by the local police—and who knows how long it would take for them to get there? Most motels are only one or two stories. This makes it very easy for criminals to break into your room. If you must stay at a motel, try to stay on the upper floor close to the front office. Make sure there are outside lights right by your door, and your car is parked close by in a well-lit area. Of course, call on your intuition to tell you which is the safest spot.

Jeepers, Creepers, Make Sure to Use Your Peepers

Whether you're staying in a motel or a hotel, always look around before you enter your room. Make sure no one is following you.

If you're concerned, immediately go back to the front desk or manager's office and get an employee to escort you to your room. *A savvy Safety Chick is never afraid to ask for help.* Do not leave your room before looking outside, either through the peephole or out the window. If someone is lurking, call the front desk or wait for the stranger to leave. I cannot impress upon you enough that you need to listen to your intuition. It is vital to your personal safety, especially when traveling alone.

Registering

Remember how you filled out your luggage tag? Well, once again, never use your first name. When filling out the registration card, put either J. Jones or Mr. and Mrs. Jones. Look, I'm as independent as the next gal, but you don't want to advertise that you are a woman staying alone. It just isn't worth the risk.

When the clerk is giving you your room key, ask him not to announce the number. Have him write it on a piece of paper and hand it to you. While you're there, instruct the front desk never to give out your name or room number. If someone inquires about you, ask for the clerk to call you in your room and tell you who it is. Don't leave your credit card lying on the counter; hand it directly to the front desk clerk, and make sure he returns the right credit card to you.

And watch your back. Many a con has been pulled at the front desks of hotels, with a criminal either lurking behind you to copy down your credit card information, or to steal your purse or bags while you are busy registering.

Location, Location, Location
Request a room from the fourth to the sixth floor that does not have a connecting door. Did you know that many fire de-

partment ladders will not reach beyond the sixth floor? Anything lower than the fourth floor, or a room with adjoining door, is easier accessibility for criminals. Anything higher than the sixth floor not only could be a fire safety issue, but also requires more time riding up and down the elevator. (Elevator safety will be discussed later in the chapter.) Make sure your room is near a heavily trafficked area such as an elevator or a vending machine. It might be loud, but the more people milling about, the safer you are. Criminals like to strike in isolated areas where they can carry out their crimes unnoticed and undisturbed.

Staying in Your Hotel

Ask to be escorted to your room, either by a bellman or front desk clerk. As you walk to your room, make note of where the emergency exits are, as well as fire alarms and extinguishers. When you arrive at your room, ask the bellman or clerk to wait while you check the room. Check to make sure there is no one in the room—under the bed, in the closet, or the bathroom. Make sure that the telephone, deadbolts, locks, and windows are functioning and that the door closes securely. Once you have established that everything is in working order, tip the nice bellman and unpack your bags. (Don't forget to lock your valuables in the hotel safe upon arrival.) Put that safety flashlight and battery-operated alarm clock by the bed—I know you followed the Safety Chick Checklist for Travel. Now, relax and order room service.

Who's That Knockin' On My Door?

If someone is at your door, regardless of whether you are staying at a hotel or motel, look through the peephole, and never open the door if you do not recognize the face staring back at you. If you are not expecting room service or a visitor, ask who it is and what they want. If it is someone claiming that they are from the hotel and need to work on something, ask for their name and call the front desk first. If they are who they say they are, they will not mind waiting. If it is a stranger, tell them you do not want to be disturbed and report them to the front desk.

> Noise is a great crime deterrent. Put a lamp or chair in front of your hotel door and window or objects that make a racket if knocked over during an attempted break-in.
>
> —from SecurityWorld.com

Giving Me the Sign

Once you have freshened up and want to go out and see the sights, make sure you take your room key, matchbook or hotel business card, and any money or valuables that you did not lock in the hotel safe. When you leave your room, leave on the television and put a Do Not Disturb sign on your door. If thieves think that someone is in the room, they are less likely to try to break in while you're gone.

Going Up?

As you are making your way down to the lobby, when the elevator doors open, don't enter if there's just one other person inside. Remember: safety in numbers. While it's fun to fantasize about the elevator scene with Michael Douglas and Glenn Close in *Fatal Attraction*, in reality strangers can be trouble. (Remember how the movie ended?) Wait for another car instead of taking your chances with a stranger.

If you find yourself in a potentially violent situation, press several buttons so the car will stop at each floor, allowing you to get out as soon as you can.

Safe R & R

If you decide to get some rest and relaxation by the pool, first put your cocktail flag up to signal the waitress that you would like to order a nice, cool beverage; then pull out your magazines. If you've brought the magazines from home, be sure to tear off the mailing label and rip it up into tiny pieces so no one can get hold of your personal address.

Most hotel personnel find it refreshing when people initiate their own personal safety. Do not be embarrassed or paranoid about following these safety tips. In most cases, you will find that the hotel staff will be extremely accommodating and think of you as a savvy, empowered Safety Chick.

Where the Hell Am I?

How to get around in a strange town without looking like a target . . . I mean, tourist

Exploring a new city is a wonderful experience. Finding a fabulous restaurant or cool boutique is always a thrill. But your status as a tourist does not have to be tattooed on your forehead. If you have been paying attention to the first part of this chapter, then you already know that the key to being safe is to be inconspicuous. This means no sparkly diamonds, no sassy clothing, and no big wads of money being flashed around. You have your money and traveler's checks safely tucked in your sensible purse and all your valuables are either at home or locked in the hotel safe. Okay, now you're ready to do some sightseeing.

You Can Tell by the Way I Use My Walk . . .

"Plan your dive, dive your plan." Know where you are going and exactly how to get there. Remember, before you leave your hotel, ask the concierge or front desk clerk how to get to your destination. If you need to look at a map, wait until you step into a coffee shop or store to open it. There is no bigger crime target than the little lost soul . . . staring at her map dazed and confused in the middle of the sidewalk. When you are walking down the street, act like you know where you are going. (Do not do the Mary Tyler Moore thing and spin around in the middle of the street in awe of all the big buildings.) The best criminals strategically plan who their victims are; most street thugs who are interviewed will tell you that they look for those who look scared or unfamiliar with their surroundings. Your best defense is *confidence*. When you're out on the street, stand up straight, walk with a purpose, and keep a hand on your purse.

Dress for Success

I'm sure you are a hip and hot woman, but try not to accentuate your positives by wearing revealing clothing. There is definitely a time and a place for that cute little sun dress and those strappy sandals, but your best bet when visiting a strange city is to dress conservatively with comfortable walking shoes. I am not suggesting that you need to dress frumpy, just don't look like you stepped out of the pages of Frederick's of Hollywood, especially if you are traveling alone. Sex offenders prey on women who are unsure of their surroundings and who are wearing "easily accessible" clothing such as short skirts, dresses, or overalls (the straps are quickly cut with a knife or razor blade).

Mind Your Manners

When you are out in public, be respectful and courteous. Speak in a low, confident tone. There is nothing worse than the loud, rude tourist who is completely oblivious to everyone and everything around her. When I was visiting in Germany, I was standing behind an American woman who was trying to change some currency. The polite bank teller began speaking to her in German. The American woman started screaming at her, "Do I look German to you?" and demanded that the teller speak English. People like that bring the term "Ugly American" to life. Be respectful of the city or country that you are visiting. You never know—if a local doesn't appreciate your behavior, you might find yourself in a sticky situation.

When traveling with your children, dress them alike (if they'll let you) so they are easy to spot and you have an exact description of what they were wearing in case they get lost. Also, keep a color picture of their faces in your wallet for identification purposes as well as for a quick fix of their cuteness.

Say "Cheese"

I love family photos. My kids cringe when we are visiting somewhere new because I make them pose at every landmark. (You'd think I was asking them to eat brussels sprouts.) The fact is, it's wonderful to have the memories documented. However, don't get so caught up in getting the perfect shot that you aren't aware of your surroundings. Don't put your purse down while you take the picture of the Statue of Liberty only to have some crook run by and grab your valuables. Be suspicious of an eager person offering to take the picture for you; you'd be amazed how quickly that "nice" person can disappear with your camera.

Making New Friends

When you are traveling alone, part of the fun is meeting people. Whether it's work related or in a museum, you don't have to be completely anti-social to be safe. Use your common sense and intuition when out in public. If you meet someone, avoid giving the new acquaintance any personal information. Stick to less personal topics of conversation and whatever you do, *don't talk politics*. Seriously, when socializing with strangers, stay in an open, public place. Never go back to "their place" or to a secluded spot with them—even if the stranger is a babe. Remember Ted Bundy? If you want to get to know him or her better, agree to meet for dinner at a crowded restaurant. Do not tell the person where you are staying—give a general response instead. An example would be, "I'm staying at a place across town, let's just meet at the museum." When you are ready to go home, get in a taxi—*by yourself*. If a romance is going to bud, save it for when you get home and can take the time to let it happen.

Out and About

Parking lots and garages are favorite places for criminals to strike. If you have a rental car, valet park whenever you can. If you must park in a garage, make sure it is in a well-lit area close to the parking attendant or entrance. Secure the lock and don't leave any of your personal belongings inside. Important business documents or personal items should be left in your hotel or locked in the trunk. If your hotel/motel requires you to have a sign on your dashboard for parking on their property, remove it from the dash while you are out and replace it when you return.

Whether you are traveling with your family, friends, or alone, these safety tips will greatly reduce your risk of becoming another "accidental tourist." Enjoy the freedom of traveling around the country or abroad, but take the time to follow these easy, common-sense security measures. Going everywhere with confidence and style—that's definitely the Safety Chick way.

The SAFETY CHICK Checklist

IMPORTANT ITEMS FOR TRAVEL

- ☑ Flashlight
- ☑ Prescription medications
- ☑ First-aid kit
- ☑ Battery-operated alarm clock
- ☑ Prepaid calling card
- ☑ A list of emergency contacts
- ☑ A copy of your itinerary
- ☑ A copy of your passport and an extra passport photo
- ☑ Copies of your driver's license, insurance information, and credit card numbers

Chapter 3

Party Girl, Watch Your Cocktail

How to Protect Yourself from Being Slipped a Mickey Out on the Town

When I was a junior at UCLA, I attended many fraternity parties, but one particular party will always stand out—and not because I hooked up with the man of my dreams. I still remember the house. It had a steep flight of stairs in front, and it was one of the most popular houses on Fraternity Row. I went with some of my Delta Gamma sorority sisters and was ready for a night of fun.

At the beginning of the party, a guy I had never met handed me a clear plastic cup with some form of cocktail in it. Trusting college coed that I was, I drank it. That's it—only one cocktail the entire night. A while later, when I was on the dance floor, it felt like my high heels had turned into roller skates and my legs were rubber bands. The nice frat boy who had given me the drink generously offered to walk me home. As I slid down the steep flight of steps, I started to realize that things were not going well. As we entered my apartment, I flung myself into the bathroom and began what would be a long night of "praying to the porcelain god."

Everything began to get really fuzzy, but I remember the nice frat boy trying to take off my clothes. (We won't even mention how desperate he must have been to want to get it on with a plastered girl with disgusting breath.) Anyway, the next thing I remember was my roommate grabbing the guy by the back of the neck and screaming at him to "Get the hell out of our apartment!" If my truly wonderful roommate had not walked in at that very moment, I hate to think what would have happened.

Look, I love a great party just as much as the next gal, but in this day and age, getting slipped a Mickey is all too common. According to the Department of Justice, in the year 2000 alone, there were over 1,500 emergency room incidents involving the drug gamma hydroxybutyrate (GHB), up from 56 in 1994. This is just one of the many types of "club drugs" that have become increasingly popular at all-night dance parties, or raves, as the hip chicks like to call them. Raves are large parties held in warehouses, nightclubs, and even open fields. They usually include loud, rapid-tempo "techno" music and light shows, smoke or fog machines, and pyrotechnics. Roofies (rohypnol), ecstasy (MDMA), and liquid ecstasy (GHB) are some of the most dangerous recreational drugs to be found at raves. Users report that the drugs heighten their perception, especially their visual stimulation. Quite often users will dance with light sticks and use Vicks Vapo Rub to enhance the physical effects of the drugs. It seems that sexual assault is becoming one of the most prevalent side effects of these drugs; therefore, every safe party Chick needs to be aware of these dangers and protect her cocktail!

There are some important tips to take from the story at the

beginning of this chapter. Never accept a drink from someone you don't know. Always party with a buddy. Finally, if you or anyone you know is even *thinking* about using any of these drugs, heed Nancy Reagan's warning and Just Say No!

Types of Club Drugs

In order for you to know what to say no to, you need to be educated on what these drugs look like, taste like, and do. The Safety Chick, along with help from the experts at the Drug Enforcement Administration in the Department of Justice, will give you the lowdown on this very dangerous trend.

Rohypnol (flunitrazepam)

STREET NAMES: Roofies, Rophies, Roche, Forget-me-pill, Circles, Mexican Valium, Rib, Roach-2, Roopies, Rope, Ropies, Ruffies, and Roaches

Rohypnol is most commonly known as "the date-rape drug." One of the significant effects of the drug is anterograde amnesia, which means you can't remember anything after taking the drug until you regain conciousness, a factor that strongly contributed to its inclusion in the Drug-Induced Rape Prevention and Punishment Act of 1996. It is available in a 0.5-milligram and 1-milligram oblong tablet as well as an injectable solution. Roche Pharmaceuticals phased out the 2-milligram dose tablet between 1996 and 1997 and is also phasing out the round, white 1-milligram tablet. The new pill will be an oblong tablet, olive green in color, and imprinted with the number 542. The new tablet includes a dye which, according to the manufacturer, will turn green if slipped into a drink.

Other effects of the drug can be decreased blood pressure, drowsiness, visual disturbances, dizziness, confusion, nausea, vomiting, and urinary retention. Users of the drug report effects similar to alcohol intoxication but claim that they wake up in the morning without a hangover.

MDMA (3, 4-methylenedioxymethamphetamine)
STREET NAMES: Ecstasy, XTC, E, X, and Adam

Ecstasy is synthetic and has a psychoactive substance possessing stimulant and mild hallucinogenic properties. Also known as the "feel good drug" or "hug drug," it reduces your inhibitions, eliminates anxiety, and makes you extremely empathetic with others and extremely relaxed. The pills also reportedly suppress the desire to eat, drink, and sleep. They are not legally manufactered and are produced in tablet, gel cap, and powder form. Tablets are often stamped with a cartoon character or Nike swoosh and come in a variety of colors. This drug causes damage to the neurons (nerve cells) that utilize serotonin to communicate with other neurons in the brain. Recreational MDMA users risk permanent brain damage that may manifest itself in depression, anxiety, memory loss, learning difficulties, and other neuropathic disorders. A smart and safe Chick would not risk subjecting herself to any of that.

GHB (gamma hydroxybutyrate)
STREET NAMES: Liquid Ecstasy, Soap, Easy Lay, Georgia Home Boy, Grievous Bodily Harm, Liquid X, and Goop

GHB is a central nervous system depressant that was banned by the FDA in 1990. It originally was sold in health food stores as a releasing agent for growth hormones that would stimulate muscle growth. GHB is highly soluble, so it is often added to bottled water or concealed in mouthwash bottles. At lower doses, GHB causes drowsiness, dizziness, nausea, and visual disturbances. At higher doses, unconsciousness, seizures, severe respiratory depression, and coma can occur. As of January 2000, the DEA had documented 60 GHB-related deaths and that figure is rising.

As a recreational drug, GHB reportedly generates feelings of euphoria and intoxication. It is mostly found in liquid form. It has a salty taste, so flavorings are sometimes added, and the drug may be disguised as a high-carbonated health drink. GHB is often added to alcoholic beverages, which can enhance the effect of the drug but also increases the potential for respiratory distress. This drug has been used in many sexual assaults because it may render victims incapable of resisting and can cause memory problems that complicate the prosecution process.

GBL (gamma butyrolactone) is a chemical used in many industrial cleaners and is the precursor chemical for the manufacture of GHB. Believe it or not, some partygoers drink small quantities of GBL straight because it is synthesized by the body to produce a GHB-type feeling. This also can cause a severe physical reaction (violent regurgitation of the fluid), increase the effects of alcohol, and cause respiratory distress, seizures, coma, and death.

Ketamine

STREET NAMES: K, Special K, and Cat Valium

This drug originally was marketed as a general anesthetic for human and veterinary use. Press reports have stated that veterinary clinics have been robbed specifically for their ketamine stock. The euphoric, hallucinogenic effects of ketamine are similar to that of LSD or phencyclidine (PCP). The drug can cause delirium, amnesia, depression, long-term memory loss, and fatal respiratory problems. The liquid can be injected into the bloodstream, poured into a drink, or applied to a smokable product like a cigarette or pipe. The powder looks similar to cocaine; it, too, can be smoked, injected, or put into drinks. Due to ketamine's ability to make someone unconscious yet still breathing it is also used as a date-rape drug.

For more in-depth information on these and other drugs, refer to the Drug Abuse Warning Network (DAWN). See the Resource Guide for contact information.

If You Need to Powder Your Nose, Bring Your Drink

And other wise tips on protecting your cocktail

There are a few very important steps to follow to avoid being drugged unwittingly.

Never leave your drink unattended. If you have to use the restroom, bring your drink; if you hit the dance floor, bring your drink; if you are immersed in conversation, hold your drink; if you have to make a phone call, take your drink. Get the idea? Don't rely on your friends to watch your beverage. All it takes is one distraction—a cute guy walking by, for example—for someone to sneak the drug into your drink. If you think your drink has been left unattended, don't take the chance; throw it away and get a new one.

Never take a drink from a stranger. My story at the beginning of this chapter should be testament enough. If possible, get a beverage that you can open yourself, such as bottled water, soda, or beer.

Never drink out of an open punch bowl. Spiking a punch bowl used to mean sneaking in a flask of your parents' alcohol to the school dance. It now takes on a whole new meaning. Opt for the sealed beverage and skip the punch.

Don't drink out of a container that is being passed around. Just the thought of this grosses me out! Despite the obvious germs that can be exchanged, you never know what has been slipped into the beverage.

If your drink tastes funny, get rid of it. If your drink has been tainted, it might taste salty or have unusual foam or residue around the top. Sometimes it has a blue color, but if it is a dark drink you won't be able to see it. Use your intuition: If you have any doubt, pour it out.

What to Do if You Have Been Drugged

You might not feel anything for 15 to 30 minutes; the first noticeable signs might be dizziness, drowsiness, confusion, impaired motor skills, disorientation, or disinhibition. If you suddenly feel like this and you've only had one or two cocktails, beware. The first thing to do is tell a friend who is with you. Have this person help you to a safe place and stay with you at all times.

Drink Safe Technology, founded by Franciso Guerra and Dr. Brian Glover, has created a date-rape drug test kit. This coaster-shaped test pad changes color to tell if your drink has been contaminated. For more info go to www.drinksafetech.com

If you start feeling extremely ill, get to a hospital or call 911 for help. According to the Rape Treatment Center in Santa Monica, California, these drugs metabolize very quickly in your body. The sooner you get medical attention, the better chance you have of finding out what you were drugged with. Request a urine test; rohypnol and GHB are easily detected in urine, and the hospital can run special tests that can detect them. If you have been drugged with rohypnol, there is a reversing agent called romazicon that can be administered by a doctor.

"Would You Like to See My Etchings?"

The easiest way to get out of an uncomfortable sexual setting is to not be there in the first place

One of the most important ways to avoid becoming a victim of rape is to avoid compromising situations. Be very careful if you have been drinking or using drugs. Your judgment will be clouded. If you do find yourself in an uncomfortable situation, follow these guidelines from the Rape Treatment Center Web site (look for the address in the Resource Guide), and get out of there!

> **Remember: Acquaintance rape is a crime.** It is never okay for someone to use force in sexual situations, no matter what the circumstances are.
>
> **Know your sexual intentions and limits.** Some men think that drinking heavily, dressing provocatively, or agreeing to be alone with them indicates a willingness to have sex. Be extremely careful to communicate your limits and

intentions clearly before you get into a situation you can't get out of. You have the right to say no to any unwanted sexual contact. If you aren't sure about what you want, communicate with your partner; ask him to respect your feelings.

Communicate your limits firmly and directly. "NO" means "NO." Say it like you mean it. Do not give mixed signals to your partner. Back up your words with a firm voice and clear body language.

Don't be afraid to "make waves" if you feel threatened. If you feel you are being pressured or coerced into sexual activity against your will, don't hesitate to state your feelings and get out of the situation. A few minutes of social awkwardness or embarrassment is better than the trauma of a sexual assault.

According to the National Center for Victims of Crime, 80 percent of the women who are raped are assaulted by someone they know.

Attend large parties with friends you can trust. Agree to look out for one another. Try to leave with a group, rather than alone or with someone you don't know well.

What to Do If You Have Been Raped

If you have been the victim of a sexual assault, get to a safe place and call the police. Have a trusted friend stay with you and help you through this devastating and horrific time. Make sure to preserve all physical evidence of the assault. Do not take a shower, do not change your clothes, do not wash your hands or brush your teeth. If you suspect you were drugged, find the glass or bottle you were drinking from—but only if it is safe to do so. Every speck of evidence should be collected at the hospital by law enforcement professionals. Write down as much as you can remember of the incident and the description of the rapist. Make sure you do it right after the event, so little details are still fresh in your mind. The more evidence you have the easier it will be convict the scumbag who did this to you. Get emotional support—there are wonderful rape crisis centers all over the country (refer to the Resource Guide at the end of the book) that can assist you in getting the help that you need.

According to a recent study conducted by the National Institute on Alcohol Abuse and Alcoholism, drinking by college students contributes to an estimated 70,000 cases of sexual assault or date rape each year, as well as 500,000 injuries and 1,400 student deaths.

The Morning After

Being raped is an extremely traumatic and life-changing event. Worrying about becoming pregnant does not have to be included in that trauma. Dr. Gary Toig, OB/GYN of Redwood City, California, recommends that any woman who has been raped call her gynecologist and the police immediately. After an exam, your doctor or other health care professional can administer pills called Preven or Plan B. These are also known as "the morning after" pills. They prevent pregnancy before it begins; it is not the same as abortion. Plan B basically contains progestin which is a hormone that works by temporarily stopping the release of an egg from a woman's ovary, or it attempts to prevent fertilization. Correct use of Plan B after unprotected sex reduces the risk of pregnancy by 89 percent. Talk with your doctor or a physician in the emergency room about these products. They are a simple way to ease concern of additional trauma.

Post-Traumatic Stress Syndrome

Post-traumatic stress disorder (PTSD) is a condition that people can get after they have been through a life-threatening experience or in a situation where they are exposed to extreme fear, horror, or grief. This emotional syndrome can manifest in different ways.

After I was kidnapped, I felt fine—or so I thought. I was badly shaken, but went about my daily life as if nothing had happened . . . until I started having flashbacks. Every day at about 4:00 in the afternoon, I would get a chill down my spine and imagine the stalker walking around the corner of my living room. This went on for weeks. I also developed a fear of flying that I never had before. It wasn't until I talked to a counselor that I realized that my feelings were valid and that I was suffering from post-traumatic stress. After realizing that I was suffering from an actual condition, I started focusing on what was making me feel so vulnerable and uneasy. I made myself relax and let my guard down. I communicated to the people closest to me how I was feeling. Gradually, the anxiety started to lessen and I began to feel somewhat like my old self again. Don't get me wrong, my life has changed since the kidnapping, but I am still me—just stronger and wiser.

If you or someone you know is suffering from post-traumatic stress syndrome, get help. Talk to a counselor or therapist. Go online and learn more about this condition. And check the Resource Guide on page 203 for Web site addresses on this subject.

Who's Your Buddy?

Always use the buddy system when you're out on the town

Always have a designated "sober" person when you go to parties, nightclubs, or any social situation. Make sure you have a "team meeting" before you leave. "Plan your dive, dive your plan"—the same motto holds true for party girls. Have fun, but always have a buddy—someone who checks up on you, and who you check on throughout the night. A friend is not a policeman, but someone who is looking out for your best interest. Plan to check in with each other every half-hour or so; at the end of the night, arrange a meeting place to convene before going home.

A Friend Is Someone Who:

Doesn't let her friends drive drunk. If any of your friends have had a few too many, do not let them drive. Call a cab or drive them home yourself.

Doesn't let her friend go home with the stranger at the bar. No matter how cute and sexy he is, you just can't trust a stranger. Encourage your friend to get the guy's phone number and call him the next day. Besides, Safety Chicks aren't slutty. If the guy's worth it, he'll wait for your call.

Gets her friend immediate medical attention if she appears to be dangerously intoxicated. If your friend seems smashed after only a few drinks, if she passes out or seems to have trouble breathing, or if she's not behaving like her normal self, get medical attention. Even if she drank too much alcohol and is just really intoxicated, she needs help. People have died from consuming too much alcohol.

Warns her friend about high-risk situations, such as clubs where "dosings" have occurred. If you have heard that a club, party, or frat house has been known to put drugs into drinks, tell your friends and suggest another location to socialize. If you see or hear that someone is "dosing" a drink or punch bowl, intervene. Confront the person, warn potential victims, discard the drinks, and call the police. If your intuition tells you that the setting is dangerous, grab your friends and get out.

According to Francisco Guerra of Drink Safe Technology, 60 percent of convicted date rapists who used GHB on their victims were bartenders.

Always trusts her friends' intuition as well as her own. The more intuition, the better; if any of your friends raise a concern, listen to them. Make safety decisions together. If you feel strongly about something, communicate your concerns. Chicks work collectively to avoid trouble.

Enjoying a night out with the girls is one of the most liberating experiences for a woman, and you know and I know that there's not enough of those. By sharing how to be safe, I am not suggesting that you should don a habit and go live in a nunnery. But the reality of the world we live in these days requires that a truly liberated Safety Chick must work and play with strength and common sense.

50	a girl's gotta do . . .

The SAFETY CHICK Checklist

WHAT TO DO IF YOU'VE BEEN RAPED

☑ Get to a safe place and call the police or rape crisis center—911 Police emergency or RAINN; (800) 656-4673.

☑ Save all evidence—clothing, beverages, cups or containers.

☑ Do not touch your body—don't bathe, wash your hands, comb your hair, or do anything that will erase possible evidence.

☑ Get to a hospital emergency room and call your gynecologist—ask about the morning-after pill.

☑ Get emotional support—family, friends, rape crisis center, Post-Traumatic Stress Disorder Alliance, or other resources listed at the end of this book.

Chapter 4

Beauty Night

How to Feel Safe
When It's Girls' Night In

The husband's working late, the kids are at a sleepover. What better time to take a nice, warm bubble bath, condition your hair, do your nails, and get caught up on some reading? Then, you hear a noise. It turns out to be the cat digging through the trash, but now you can't get that shower scene from Psycho *out of your mind. What should be a joyful, relaxing evening alone suddenly turns into a night filled with paranoia and fright. Instead of relishing the tranquil serenity, you end up wishing your screaming children and spouse would hurry up and get home.*

Women always ask me, "How do you sleep at night? I can't stand it when my husband's away!" Or, "When my roommate works late, I usually go to a friend's house. I'm too scared to stay in my apartment by myself." This drives me crazy! Even I got tired of feeling terrified in the comfort of my own home. My favorite thing in the world is taking a relaxing bubble bath, and I'll be damned if some creepy guy is going to take that away from me. I deserve to feel safe in my own home, and so do you!

I went to great lengths to learn about home security products and really researched my different choices. In this chapter I share with all you aspiring Safety Chicks out there the vital tools you need to feel more comfortable when you are home alone or anytime. A year-2000 statistical study of crime in America from the Department of Justice shows that 75 percent of the crimes involved property theft. Despite this, there are plenty of things you can do to avoid becoming one of the 19.3 million people who are affected.

If I'm Home a Rockin', Don't Come a Knockin'

Tips for dealing with strangers on your doorstep

The number one rule when you're home alone is: Do not answer your door unless you know who's there—for example, a friend or family member. Mail delivery such as FedEx or UPS will usually leave packages at your doorstep. (You should not be receiving packages at your home address, in the first place: See chapter 6, Guys Who Won't Take *No* for an Answer.)

Ban the Fuller Brush Man

Strangers who sell magazine subscriptions or other products door-to-door are in the wrong business. Tell these salesmen, "Thank you, but I don't do any business at the door," then shut and lock the door. In this day and age, there are so many solicitors in on a scam, that you just can't take the chance. The problem is that anyone can get a fraudulent ID, and it's almost impossible to tell the valid ones from the fake. Little Janie, the Girl Scout, is a whole different story. Chances are, if they are in the 8 to 10 age range and are wearing a Girl Scout uniform, they're good for a box of Thin Mints. On the other hand, the young adult trying to win a trip to Disneyland by selling subscriptions just isn't a good bet.

While many of these solicitors are legitimate, there are more who are not. If you want to help a teen or other charitable organization, donate your time or money, but not at your front door.

> "At the worst, a house unkept cannot be so distressing as a life unlived."
> —Rose Macaulay

Sign of the Times

A good way to discourage unwanted solicitors at *all* times is to put up a sign. Any local hardware store or stationary store should carry a plaque that says NO SOLICITORS. A BEWARE OF DOG sign can also be a deterrent—whether you have a pet or not. If unwanted salesmen still approach, they are too aggressive, and it's best not to answer the door.

Who's That Knockin' on My Door?

The bottom line is: Always look through your peephole or window to see who is there before you answer the door. If it is absolutely necessary for you to open the door and you are home alone (like when you're waiting for a repairman) a good tactic is to yell, "Don't worry, honey, I'll get it." At least, you're projecting the impression that someone is home with you. Better yet, if you need to have an appliance repaired or utility turned on, make sure that you are home and always have a friend or spouse there with you. If you live in an apartment, make it clear to your manager or superintendent that you must be notified ahead of time before anyone enters your home. All companies should be bonded and insured.

Baby, I've Got Your Number

You do not have to talk to anyone who calls you just because they dialed your number. The telemarketing world has been hit hard by the public realizing that once they have told a company not to call, it is illegal for that telemarketing business to disturb them again. When answering the phone, just say, "Hello." Do not give your name or number. If you receive a wrong number and the caller asks what number he has reached, respond by asking him who and what number he was trying to reach. Do not give out unnecessary personal information to strangers, and please: Never tell a stranger you are home alone. The best way to handle the phone when you are alone is not at all. Put the answering machine on, and RELAX.

Apartment Dwellers

For those of you who live in an apartment, dormitory, or condominium, make sure you have a wide-angle peephole in your front door. Do not depend on a chain lock to keep out unwanted visitors. Question the person through the door, *not* face to face. Try not to rent an apartment that does not have a secure entrance with an intercom system. A lobby with a security guard is best. Encourage all tenants to keep the outer main doors locked at all times. Do not let a stranger enter the building while you are coming or going. Tell them they must check in through the intercom system first. If you see someone trying to enter the building covertly, notify the security guard or police.

The last thing you want to do when you have just settled into to your warm bath is to get out and answer the phone or door. Make the decision: Beauty Night is *your* night—don't let anyone ruin it.

Snug as a Bug in a Rug

How to make your home secure, outside and in

Your property should be secure at all times, whether you're home or not. Adequate security can prevent thieves from being tempted to target your house. Burglars look for opportunities. By removing easy opportunities, you remove yourself from becoming a prospective victim. For example, according to the FBI, simply displaying an alarm decal from your security company on the front window can reduce your chance of being burglarized by 76 percent. What an easy way to deter a thief! There are community officers in most police stations who will come to your home and teach you how to make your property more secure. Call your local department to find out if they offer this service. Follow these easy tips so your house becomes a bad choice for a burglar.

Outside Security

The Perimeter
The first step is to walk around the outside of your property—with your Safety Chick Checklist from page 67 in hand—and make a note of everything that needs to be corrected. Remove any plants or shrubs that obscure the entrance to your home. Make sure you can see your door clearly from the street. Officers who patrol your neighborhood need to be able to view your property from their cars. Plants that screen the entrance of your home make it possible for robbers to break in without being seen. Hedges or bushes around your house make perfect hiding places for criminals. The back of the house should be clear as well. If you have a separate garage, keep the path clear from the garage to the back door.

A Thorn on Your Side

Plant thorny bushes, such as roses or bougainvillea, under windows and along fences; this puts someone trying to break and enter in a "stick-y" situation. It also deters an intruder from hopping the fence onto your property.

Lock It Up

If you have a fence on the side of the house that leads to the rear of the property, make sure there is a secure latch on the gate door. For night protection or added security, place a padlock on the inside of the gate latch.

Clean Up after Yourself

If you or the hubby have been doing a little fixing up around the house, make sure to put all ladders and tools away when you're finished. A ladder leaning against the house or a tool left by a window is quite helpful to the burglar trying to enter your home.

Light Up Your Life

Sensor lights are an essential part of the exterior of your home. Not only are they helpful when you come home at night, but if someone is lurking on your property, nothing shocks them more than a light popping on and blowing their cover. Sensor lights can be found at any hardware or lighting store. They come in various sizes and ranges of distance and are easy to install. (This Safety Chick has installed them herself.) Place them in the front, back, and sides of your home to detect movement all around the property.

The Doors

I'm not referring to the band; I'm talking about the gateway to your home. While front doors with etched glass are beautiful, they are also a burglar's dream. Forget picking the lock. They just break the glass, reach their hand in and unlock the door. Opt for a wooden door with a solid core; many of them come beautifully etched as well.

Be a Dead-Head
Make sure that all of your locks are deadbolts that extend at least one inch and are made of steel. If you have French doors, use a key as opposed to a knob lock on the inside, and keep the key handy in case of fire or other emergency. Do *not* leave the key in the lock. The glass should be double-paned.

Put Vaseline or some other clear lubricant on the surface of drainpipes that are close to windows. This gives a burglar quite a surprise as he's trying to shinny up the pipe to get into your second-story window.

Kick My Door, I Dare Ya!
Even with a solid deadbolt, thieves can still kick in a door. So to be extra se-cure, there are a couple of reinforce-ments you should install along with your locks. These are called strike plates and door reinforcers. According to the *National Locksmith* publication, a MAG High Security Box Strike combined with the Don-Jo wraparound plate and Schlage B600 series deadbolt were impenetrable even when a fork-lift rammed the door.

The Key to a Safe Home
There are some wonderful products out there that provide a re-mote, keyless entry for security and convenience. These look like the remote keypad you use to lock your car doors. Most are equipped with a Rolling Code security with billions of access

combinations, so it never uses the same code twice. There is a keyless deadbolt available on Securerite.com that is compatible with a Genie Intellicode garage door opener, so you need only one keypad to open your garage and house.

There are some wireless keys that can turn on and off your house lights as well. Another electronic key solution is the e-res, which is a "smart key." The e-res system operates with a small computer inside that allows you to store and receive information about where and when the key has been used. The great thing about these "smart keys" is that you never have to change your locks. You just add or delete a user, and the key cannot be duplicated. This is a great idea if you have rental property or an apartment situation with a bunch of roommates.

Finally, do not hide an extra key under the doormat, in the mailbox, or under the flowerpot. Thieves know that those are the most common places to hide a key. Opt for a "hide-a-rock" that blends in with the yard, or another not-so-obvious location.

Inside Security

Please Leave a Message . . .

While it's tempting to leave a clever message on your answering machine, the safe thing is to have a generic voice, preferably male, stating simply to please leave a message at the tone. Do not leave any details of your whereabouts on the recording, and please: Do not state that you live alone or are not at home.

The Window to Your Soul

All of the windows in your home should have locks on them, preferably a double-cylinder lock with a key, regardless of how small the opening. Think of intruders as rodents; they can squeeze through anything.

You can prevent an intruder from opening a window by inserting screws or wooden dowels into the frame or track. For example, if you have a double-hung window: Drill a hole at an angle through the bottom of the top window and into the top of the bottom window, then insert a metal pin or carriage bolt that can easily be removed when you want to open the window. For sliding windows, get a wooden dowel or metal rod that fits tightly in the track when the window is shut, and can be removed when opened. Sliding glass doors should be treated the same way: rod in track and—of course—double-paned. Those louvered windows are an intruder's dream. Remove them and replace with a more secure style of window. IN CASE OF FIRE: If you use a cylinder lock, always remember to leave a key next to a window in every bedroom and in one window on every floor of your house day and night when you are home. Make sure they are easily accessible in case of emergency.

Always leave a little cash on a table or chair by the entrance of your home when you leave. If the cash is gone when you return, quietly leave the house and call the police. Of course, make sure to tell *all* members of the family what you are doing, so no little fingers innocently slip the money into their pockets.

It's Curtains for You

Draw your curtains, draperies, or blinds at night whether you're home or not. When it's dark outside and the lights are on, the interior of your home looks like a fishbowl from the street—perfect for an observing eye. All windows should have some type of covering, whether they're visible from the street or not.

If you have venetian or horizontal blinds, make sure you adjust the angle so that light comes in, but you cannot see in, which means the blades should angle down—but, to make sure, go outside your window and look in. If you have vertical blinds, adjust them so that you see through to a blind corner or wall, or keep them shut completely.

The Trick Is in the Timer

Set some of your lights on timers. Program them to go on at different times of the day and night to make it look as if someone is always home. You can even attach a television or radio to a timer to go on for a few minutes every couple of hours to simulate a lived-in scenario.

Batten the Hatches

When you are home alone, especially at night, make sure you have double-bolted and locked all the doors and windows. Turn a few lights on in various rooms and turn on the alarm, if you have one. This is not to make you feel like a prisoner in your own home, but to let you relax with confidence that no one is lurking around your house. Eliminate doubt and worry by locking things up and feeling secure.

Room with NO View

There should be one room in your house that has one door and no window. A walk-in closet, storeroom, pantry—you get the idea. Security experts call this a safe room. In this room you need to have a flashlight, batteries, a cell phone plugged in and charged at all times, a list of emergency numbers (besides the most important one, 911), and a weapon. This can be a gun, an Air Taser (see page 186), or even a baseball bat. There should be a double-bolted lock on the inside of the door. This room is to be used if an intruder does get into your home. Immediately get to your safe room, lock the door, and dial 911. Take a deep breath, get your weapon, and stay on the phone with the police dispatcher until the patrol officers arrive.

Natural Disasters

In case of a hurricane, earthquake, or other natural disaster, in addition to a preparedness kit (such as a flashlight, batteries, AM radio) you also should have a three-day supply of canned or non-perishable food and water. That way, you are not wandering the street with looters and other criminals who come out when disaster strikes.

Protection at Your Fingertips

Keep a canister of pepper foam beside your bed (make sure it is foam and not a spray if you are using it indoors; see page 183), by the front and back doors, and on your keychain. If you ever find yourself in need of help, it's right at your fingertips. See chapter 11, Pick Your Poison, for more information on pepper sprays and foams.

How Alarming!

Tips on installing alarm systems for your home

Everybody concerned with safety should have some type of alarm system on their residence. There is quite a range of products out there. Regardless of your budget, you should be able to equip your home with an effective device for deterring break-ins. Now, this is not to say that an alarm system guarantees that your house will never be burglarized, but it certainly improves your odds.

Vali Hashemian owns Nationwide Security System, a security alarm company for home and business. He has been in the business for more than 22 years and has a vast knowledge of home protection. It was his own personal experience, however, that showed him the importance of having the proper equipment installed around his property to avoid potential break-ins.

Vali lives in an affluent neighborhood. His property is somewhat secluded and hard to see from the street. There is a security gate at the street entrance and one further down his driveway at the entrance to his house. One evening, he noticed that both gates were open when he arrived. He was the first one home and his wife and kids had been gone all day. His intuition told him that something was amiss, so he decided to immediately install security cameras all around the property. Sure enough, the next day, the cameras caught a man walking down the driveway and looking around the property.

The next morning, Vali decided to stay home and see if the guy would show up again. Like clockwork, the man reappeared and headed up the driveway toward the house. Vali walked outside and asked the man what he was doing. Startled, the stranger said he was looking for his dog. (Yeah, right.) Vali then called the police and they were able to catch the guy as he was making his escape. It was later found out that he was part of a band of vagabonds that traveled around the country, targeting homes, and robbing them when the families were away.

Had it not been for the gates and the cameras, Vali might have been the victim of a home burglary. The key is to have some system in place to warn you of an intruder. The size of your home or property does not matter. It is the precautions you take on and around your property that can make all the difference in the world.

The Basics

Most alarm companies offer a service package for a monthly fee. This package usually includes two contact sensors for your front and back doors or ground floor windows. A motion detector, a display keypad, a control unit, yard signs, window decals, and an indoor sounder usually are included. Monitors are on duty 24 hours a day; they call the police if your alarm goes off and they cannot reach you. These packages currently run about $99, plus a $26 monthly monitoring fee.

The Next Step

If you want a little more security for your home, I would add sensors on all ground-floor windows and entry doors along with a motion sensor in the main hallway and on stairs if you have them. Motion sensors detect movement and trigger an alarm if someone were to enter your home undetected; they can be bypassed on your control panel if you are home and want the ability to walk around without setting off the alarm.

The alarm companies consider sensors extra and will charge you more than the standard package. Some companies offer special deals if you order online. I found one company that has a package for $299 that includes two additional alarm contacts, a fire protection monitor, a Quick Key remote (which turns your alarm and lights on and off by a pad on a keychain), a Smart Voice sounder (which uses a voice to tell you if you have a fire or intruder), and a 24-hour-a-day monitoring service for a $26.99 monthly fee.

The Ultimate Safety Setup

If your budget allows, here is what I believe to be the most effective home security plan. Have alarm contacts on all entrance doors and have motion detectors in hallways and on stairs. Install alarmed screens on all windows; you can order these through an alarm company or most any screen and window company. That way, you can open your windows and still have your alarm active. Have all glass windows equipped with sensors that detect breakage; or you can have a film coating put on your windows that prevents the glass from shattering; this runs about $150 and up per window. Again, all of these things are added security measures and are not included in a standard alarm package. When getting estimates, at least start with these guidelines and try to work your way down.

The Panic Button

A panic button can be attached to any alarm system. You can have this around your neck or on your keychain and push it to set off your alarm whether you are inside or outside your home.

Turn That Thing Off!

If your alarm is triggered, your control panel will call your monitoring center. If you install an outdoor sounder, your neighborhood also will be alerted to an emergency at your home. If you choose not to contract for a monitoring system on a monthly basis, you can still install an outdoor sounder. The bad news is, most people think alarms are false and tend not to pay immediate attention. The good news is, sooner or later your neighbors will want that thing turned off and call the police. Either way, law enforcement will be called to your residence to check things out.

Direct Line

Some police departments offer a service in which the control panel dials the police department directly. Check with your local law enforcement office *before* you hook up your system to see if this is offered in your town. And while you're checking, ask about false alarm charges that often are levied by law enforcement agencies, particularly when bogus alarms are triggered repeatedly.

What about Rover?

Don't worry about your pet tripping the infrared sensors in your home. The alarm companies will activate the "pet alley," which is a few inches of undetected space that can be adjusted for your cat or dog. (It can be designed according to weight, say, less than 30 pounds.)

Lights, Camera, Action

In addition to sensor lights, if you suspect burglar activity around your property or if you have a definite security concern, install surveillance cameras around the perimeter. (Just ask Vali what an important move that is.) As I have mentioned previously, sensor lights can be found at most any hardware store, are easy to install, and are cost effective. Surveillance cameras are substantially more expensive. A complete observation system is available online at Radio Shack and consists of a high-resolution 12-inch monitor, one camera, and the capability of hooking up with four additional cameras. This system runs about $600, and additional cameras run about $100 more. If cameras are not in your budget, you might want to think about getting some fake cameras and mounting them in plain view around your property. The thieves don't know if they're real or not, and most are not willing to find out.

Do It Yourself

If you are in a temporary residence, or your budget doesn't allow for a service, there are systems that you can install yourself. A wireless security system runs about $150 to $200 and usually includes a controller with auto-dialer, a motion detector, two door/window sensors, a lamp module, and a handheld keychain remote. It also has the capacity for additional sensors or motion detectors if you need them.

There is another easy do-it-yourself home safety measure.

Cover all your windows with a laminate film that holds the glass together if it is broken. You can buy it at hardware or window stores. They are sold in rolls for about $6 per square foot. Remember, any deterrent is a good deterrent.

> "If your house is really a mess and a stranger comes to the door, greet him with, 'Who could have done this? We have no enemies.'"
> —Phyllis Diller

Apartment Solutions

There is a wireless motion sensor "Alarm with a Key Chain" remote that is great for apartments or dormitories because no wiring is needed, and it only runs about $40. This triggers a 108-decibel alarm if motion is detected. It has a wireless remote that can arm and disarm, and has a panic button to instantly sound the alarm.

Beware of Bark

Never underestimate the intimidating power of a dog. A nice big K-9 cruising around your property can be one of the best intruder deterrents. Robbers and stalkers don't like to deal with animals, especially barking ones who draw attention to lurking trespassers, or worse—who bite when protecting their property. If you can't get a dog, get a tape recording of a really loud, scary bark that can be played if an unwanted solicitor comes to your door.

May I Check Your References?

Take the time to get estimates and references from local alarm companies. In addition to the products they offer, make sure to ask about their service record. Make sure these companies are bonded and have insurance. It is important that if something goes wrong with your system, the company will stand behind its products. Look to the Resource Guide on page 203 for references on how to find an alarm company in your area.

All of these tips are solutions to make your home more burglar-proof so that you feel at ease when you are home alone. Strategically securing your house gives you peace of mind. Building a perimeter of safety around your property enables you to relax and enjoy your next evening of solitude.

The SAFETY CHICK Checklist
MAKING YOUR PROPERTY SECURE

☑ Remove any plants or shrubs that obscure the front of your property.

☑ Plant thorny bushes under windows and along fences.

☑ Put a padlock on the insides of gates around the property.

☑ Do not leave ladders or tools next to the house.

☑ Install sensor lights around the perimeter of the residence.

☑ Install 1-inch deadbolts on all entrance doors.

☑ Put locks on all windows.

☑ Have some type of covering on all windows.

☑ Designate and fully equip a "safe room."

☑ Install an alarm system in the house.

Chapter 5

A Girl's Gotta Shop

How to Avoid Getting Ripped Off When You're Trying to Buy

At a mall in Los Angeles in the late 1980s, there was a rash of horrible robberies. The criminals would wait under the car of an unsuspecting shopper. When the shopper was opening her car door, the criminal would take a razor blade and slice just above the person's heel, severing her Achilles tendon and causing the victim to be incapacitated. This allowed the criminal to steal all her belongings and, in some cases, her car as well. Rest assured that these violent felons were caught, but businesses at the mall suffered from the negative publicity surrounding the incidents.

Okay, that story gave even me the willies. But again, the important lessons to learn from this are, one: Always park close to the entrance of a store where it is well lit and busy with people; and two: Always be aware of your surroundings. Are you starting to notice a theme here?

There are many dangers lurking at your local shopping malls—and I don't mean the great sale on shoes that cost you your paycheck. Credit card fraud, identity theft, general theft, and carjacking are some of the hazards that you can encounter if you are not using your intuition and street smarts.

While you are running from errand to errand, store to store, scattered, and definitely not focused on what is going on around you, you may be the perfect prey for an opportunistic thief.

To generalize, thieves are lazy. They do not like to work for their money—maybe that's why they're called "thieves." The harder you make it for them, the more likely they will leave you alone and find some less savvy shoppers. Here are some ways to make it harder for the criminals.

Keep It Close to the Vest

Never leave your wallet unattended, and other ways to avoid getting robbed

Have you left your purse in the cart at the grocery store and walked a little further down the aisle to get some hamburger meat? In the middle of a sales transaction, have you left your wallet on the counter while you bent over to deal with your fussy baby in the stroller beside you? Don't do that! Always keep your purse with you. Many victims are amazed at how quickly their valuables were stolen: "I only looked away for a minute . . ." "My purse was right next to me a second ago." If you have to look away or bend over to get something, take your purse in your hand while you do it.

Running Errands

I remember the first trip to the mall with my new baby. I was so preoccupied with getting him in the car seat, the stroller folded up and put in the back, and my packages into the car that I drove away with both of my back doors wide open. Needless to say, any psycho could have jumped into my back seat. Don't let the tasks at hand distract you from being aware. Do one thing at a time, quickly and efficiently. If you are at a grocery store, always have the bag person help you out. If you have little ones with you, the more adult helping hands, the better.

Don't Handcuff Yourself with Your Packages

When walking to your car after shopping, be alert! If you have too many packages, don't try to carry them all yourself. A thief loves a target with their wrists tied up in the handles of their bags, unable to fight as the purse is ripped from their hands. Put your packages in a cart or ask a security guard to help you to your car.

A Purse Must Do More Than Match Your Shoes

Okay, there are times when your purse can be a fashion statement. If you are going to a formal event or party, the sensible purse can stay at home. But when you are going about your daily life, you really should have a purse that is efficient and hard to rip off your body. For example, those darling backpacks or purses with the little strings are cute, but not very secure. A thief can easily cut the straps without you even noticing, then disappear into a crowd. The best purses I have seen are the ones that fit across your body diagonally. Your wallet is in front of your body and easy for you to get to. The thick strap is hard to cut. Remember: Never play tug-of-war with someone who is trying to steal your purse. Avoid injury. Let it go and then scream for the police.

Says one of my clients, "I was driving with my oldest son and witnessed a young punk ride by on his bike and yank an elderly woman's purse from her shoulder. The strap broke right off. A good Samaritan in front of me saw this happen and quickly blocked the criminal with her car. The police arrived shortly thereafter, and the woman got her purse back. What struck me was how quickly the whole event occurred and how easily those little purse straps can break. It was also a good lesson for my son to see the punk taken away in handcuffs. Crime doesn't pay."

Don't Show Your Hand

If you carry your money in your pocket, keep it in your front pants pocket. It's harder for pickpockets to get to without you noticing. Avoid flashing your money in plain view. Be discreet. A big wad is tempting for any thief, and turns you into a target.

The Best Defense Is Not to Play at All

The best way to avoid getting ripped off is to take away the opportunity. This means: Do not leave items in your car. Do not leave your car unlocked, even in your own driveway. A friend of mine lives on a very private cul-de-sac. She left her purse in the car and the doors unlocked every day for a year. One morning she came out of the house to find her purse dumped on the side of her driveway, her wallet and PDA gone. Money and other items were stolen out of her car. So much for the safe, quiet neighborhood. Remember: Crime happens everywhere!

If the Worst Happens, Work Fast!

The second you realize that you have been robbed, move into action. First, call the police and file a report. Immediately cancel your credit cards. Experts say that thieves have approximately a two-hour window to use your cards before they are reported stolen or lost. The sooner you contact the credit card companies, the less damage the criminal can do. The law states that if you report the card stolen before the thief uses it, you cannot be responsible for any unauthorized charges. If you do not report the loss in time, the most you will be responsible for is $50 per card—even if the thief uses your ATM to get cash. Make an itemized list of everything that is missing—credit card numbers, your driver's license number, and any items with their monetary value attached. This helps the police with their report and makes it easier to file a claim with your insurance company.

"Excuse Me, but That's None of Your Business."

Ways to avoid becoming a victim of credit card fraud and identity theft

Many criminals do their shopping on someone else's tab. To avoid becoming a victim of credit card fraud, there are several important tips that you need to follow. Identifying "space invaders" as I discussed in chapter 1 is a great place to start. Make sure when you are making financial transactions that there are no "shoulder surfers" behind you copying your credit card, ID, or other important numbers. Your personal information such as Social Security number, driver's license number, credit cards, home address, and telephone number should be top secret. All personal information should be given out on a need-to-know basis: never to strangers, never over the phone, and never filled out on a form someone sent you in the mail.

Credit Card Fraud

The first trick to avoiding credit card fraud is to take charge of your cards. Following these simple tips will greatly reduce your chances of becoming a victim.

According-ing to www. flash.net, more than 1,000 people a day in the United States fall victim to crimes of stolen identity.

Spell It Out

As soon as you get a new credit card, write the phrase "See ID" on the back in the space that is supposed to contain your signature. You would be amazed at how many times store clerks still don't ask to see your ID. This is an added reminder for them to do so, and can be a huge deterrent to a thief trying to use your stolen card.

You Oughta Be in Pictures

One of the best security choices you can make is to have your photo and signature imprinted on the front of your credit card. Most cards these days contain a hidden hologram or secret imprint to make it harder for criminals to make new cards from a stolen credit card number, but there's nothing better than having your face on the front of the card for merchants to compare with the customer standing before them—despite the occasional bad hair day.

Did You Get a Receipt?

The easiest way for a criminal to get your credit card number is from a receipt. Credit card slips should be tucked securely in your wallet. Do not throw them away at the store. Keep your receipts for your records and always make sure you tear them up before you dispose of them.

Take Charge of Your Receipt

Never sign a blank receipt. If a clerk says, "We'll total it up and bill you later," decline the offer and purchase your things elsewhere. Make sure that the amount is accurate. Dishonest cashiers have been known to add a few items here and there on other people's tabs, conveniently taking their "freebies" home at the end of the day. Always draw a line or a circle around the amount and initial it. That way a clerk cannot tack on more charges after you leave.

Put the PIN in Your Memory Bank

Many credit card companies assign a personal identification number (PIN) to your card so that it can also be used for getting cash. Never keep your PIN with your credit card. Put it somewhere safe at home and memorize the number. (If your memory is as good as mine—don't worry, they usually aren't too long.) If you are using a cash machine, be sure to block the screen so that no one can see your code. Thieves have been known to stand across the street with binoculars to obtain that valuable information.

Less Is More

Try to limit the amount of credit cards you use. (Finally, my husband was right about something!) As tempting as it may be, multiple credit cards can get you into trouble; not only financially, but if your wallet is stolen, the thief has a better chance of running up your bills while you're trying to cancel all your cards.

Beware of the Credit Card Con

We all get a rush out of receiving a letter in the mail that says, "You've won a prize!" But, the truth of matter is, it's probably a scam. Enclosed is usually a compelling letter telling about all the fabulous prizes you've won, along with an application the sender would like you to fill out first—in order to claim your "prizes." This form may request your bank account or credit card numbers, or such personal information as your Social Security card or driver's license numbers. Don't fall for this con; leave your prize winning for the summer carnival.

"Credit cards have three dimensions: height, width, and debt."

—Shelby Friedman, comedian

Beware of the Jilted Lover

Think long and hard before you authorize someone to use your credit cards. Many a heart has been broken and credit report ruined by an ex's charging or opening new accounts on an old flame's dime. It's best to allow only your spouse—that is, one you plan to stay married to forever—to charge on your account. No matter how in love you are, the only person authorized to charge on your card or use your credit should be *you*. That goes for co-signing bank loans, as well—you don't want to be left holding the bag when the ex bails on his loan.

Check Monthly Statements with a Fine Tooth Comb

Be sure to check every monthly statement thoroughly. Look for any inconsistencies or purchases you know you didn't make. Contact your credit card company immediately if you see something that doesn't make sense or raises a red flag.

Tag Your Own Account

You can have your credit card companies put a fraud alert signal in your records. This notifies the company every time you make a transaction or if someone is applying for a new card. The cashier then will be required to call your credit card company and have you get on the phone with them and verify certain personal information (for example, mother's maiden name, password.) This might seem like a hassle when you're in a hurry, but it's worth it if someone else tries to use your card. If you're opening a new account, the company will contact you at home to verify the personal information required.

Identity Theft

Believe it or not, the biggest source of information that may lead to identity theft comes from the very people you trust with your personal data: the credit bureaus. The next easiest source is in your own backyard—your trash.

David Nielsen is an expert in the prevention of credit card fraud and identity theft. His Web site, www.fightidentitytheft.com, is a valuable resource to consumers and potential victims of fraud. After years of working in the online credit report field, he decided to share his experience and knowledge with the public. One of the actions on the top of his list to avoid creating an unwanted paper trail: shredding.

Shred It—Or Else

Criminals really do go through people's garbage to obtain receipts and other personal information. Buying a paper shredder at your local office supply store is a smart purchase to make. Did you know that it is perfectly legal for someone to go through your trash? In a U.S. Supreme Court decision, *California vs. Greenwood*, it was stated that the "expectation of privacy in trash left for collection in an area accessible to the public . . . is unreasonable."

Here is a punch list of items you should shred after their useful life has expired:

○ Address labels from junk mail and magazines
○ ATM receipts
○ Bank statements
○ Birth certificate copies
○ Cancelled and voided checks
○ Credit and charge card bills, carbon copies, sum-
maries, and receipts
○ Credit reports and histories
○ Documents containing maiden name: used by credit
card companies for security reasons
○ Documents containing passwords or PINs
○ Documents containing your name, address, tele-
phone number, and/or e-mail address
○ Documents relating to investments
○ Driver's licenses or items with a driver's license
○ Employee pay stubs
○ Employment records
○ Expired passports or visas
○ Identification cards: college IDs, state IDs, em-
ployee ID badges, military IDs
○ Investment, stock, and property transactions
○ Items with a signature: leases, contracts, letters
○ Legal documents
○ Luggage tags
○ Medical and dental records
○ Papers with a Social Security number
○ Preapproved credit card applications
○ Receipts with checking account numbers
○ Report cards
○ Résumés or curriculum vitae
○ Tax forms
○ Transcripts
○ Travel itineraries

○ **Used airline tickets**
○ **Utility bills**

If you have a large quantity of documents to shred, there are companies that will come to your home or office and securely shred all the items at once. They are able to work on a weekly, monthly, or bi-annual basis. Check out the Resource Guide on page 203 for more information.

Privacy, Please

There are information brokers whose sole business is to gather as much information about you as they can and sell it to anyone who wants it: banks, supermarkets, retailers, insurance companies, even criminals if they are willing to pay the price. Your bank, brokerage firms, credit card companies, and insurance companies are required by law to send you a "privacy notice" each year. Those companies that sell your data to third parties must tell you and give you the chance to opt out. Make sure you make it clear that you do not want your personal information sold. If you have not received a privacy notice, contact the company and ask for another form.

Treat Your Credit Report like Gold

A credit report holds the most personal and vital information anyone can have. The information contained in the report influences crucial decisions on loans, insurance coverage, employment—even housing. Although this information is supposed to remain top secret and extremely confidential (according to the Federal Fair Credit Reporting Act—FCRA), it's relatively easy for anyone to get their hands on these personal records.

One of the potential leaks of confidentiality comes from the excessive amount of "extra hands" that are involved with your report. Banks, retail stores, and credit card issuers all have outside companies managing different aspects of their businesses. Having such a large number of people with access to this data inevitably means trouble. Criminals would love to get hold of your credit report. It's the simplest way to steal your identity.

Order Your Report

The Federal Trade Commission (FTC) recommends that you look over a copy of your credit report once a year. To protect yourself even more, you might want to think about seeing your report twice a year. A lot of damage can be done in a year—just ask any victim of identity theft.

The three biggest credit bureaus are Experian (used to be known as TRW), Eqifax, and TransUnion. All you need to do is call or contact them online, and for about $8 you will receive a copy of your report. You can receive a free report if you have recently been denied credit, been a victim of fraud, are unemployed, or receive welfare benefits. Check the Resource Guide for contact information.

If You Think You Are a Victim of Identity Theft

1. **Check your credit report for any new accounts or credit inquires that have shown up.**
2. **Contact the credit card companies or banks where you have seen inconsistencies or problems.** Ask to speak to the security or fraud department. Review your account with them and highlight any incorrect charges or unauthorized business. If it is more than a billing mistake, you should close the account immediately and change all ID numbers and passwords.
3. **Contact the major check verification companies if you suspect someone has set up a bank account in your name or is using your stolen checks.** If you can pinpoint a merchant that has received one of your stolen checks, find out which verification company they use and contact that company immediately.

4. **Document all contacts.** As with all cases dealing with victimization, you need to be your own detective. Keep a notebook documenting a log of all conversations, complete with names, dates, time of call, details, and telephone numbers.

5. **Contact the fraud department of each of the three major credit bureaus.** Tell them that you think you've been a victim of identity theft and that you want them to put a "fraud alert" on your file and issue no new credit without your approval.

6. **File a police report.** Get a copy of the report for the bank, credit card company, or anyone else who might need proof that a crime was committed.

7. **File a complaint with the FTC hotline (877) 488-4338 or (877) ID-THEFT:** The FTC doesn't actually deal with the prosecution of identity theft, but it can help victims resolve financial problems that can occur as a result of the theft.

8. **Contact the Postal Inspection Service** if you think a criminal has submitted a change of address in your name or used any other postal service to commit acts of fraud.

9. **Contact the Social Security Administration** if you have reason to believe that your Social Security number is being fraudulently used.

10. **Contact the Internal Revenue Service** if you think improper use of your identity has resulted in tax violations.

Check the information on how to contact all of these organizations at the end of the book. You must work fast and be diligent. Unfortunately the credit world is not the most effective and organized. It is very easy to get frustrated and give up. The best way to stay on top is to closely read all statements and records, and to keep detailed accounts of any problems that arise. It never hurts to fire off a good, strong letter to company heads and consumer protection groups—it can help you let off a little steam and might just strike a chord with someone who can assist you.

Get Rid of the Junk

How to get your name off every annoying junk mail and telemarketing list

I cover how to handle salesmen at your door in chapter 4, but you also want to get yourself off those pesky marketing lists. I will refer to David Nielsen again to get a handle on yet another way a thief can steal your identity. He showed me how to "slow the flow," as he puts it, of junk mail and telemarketing calls.

The first thing you need to realize is that there are an incredible amount of sources where these junk mailers troll. You need to be extremely cautious every time you write down your name, address, and phone number. Warranty cards, donating to charitable organizations or clubs, and subscribing to magazines, book clubs, or music clubs all are ways your name enters the never-ending world of junk mail hell. To stay cool, you must become extremely diligent about where and to whom you reveal personal information.

To Stop the Flow of Junk Mail and Telemarketers
  1. Call the three major credit bureaus:

  The Credit Bureau's Main Opt-Out Line: (888) 567-8688
     This 30-second call to an automated voice lets you opt out of all credit-related offers for two years, or permanently.

Experian Consumer Services: (800) 407-1088

This service removes your name from noncredit offers coming off Experian lists: the root of the junk mail evil; samples, coupons, catalogs, and local or national promotional flyers. Again, it's a 30-second call to an automated response system.

Direct Marketing Association—DMA Opt-Out (for this one, you need to use snail mail): Mail Preference Service, Direct Marketing Association, P.O. Box 9008, Farmington, NY 11735-9008

This is an industry organization that puts people on a list distributed to the more reputable direct mail companies. It puts you on a "do not want to receive" list for national catalogs and marketing companies. The problem is that many companies don't update their mailing lists for three to six months, so it might take a while before you see any big changes in your junk mail volume.

According to Fight identity theft.com, about 62 million trees and 25 billion gallons of water are used to produce a typical year's worth of junk mail in the United States.

Or, notify all three major credit bureaus by dialing one number: (888) 567-8688 or 5-OPT-OUT: This gets your name off mailing lists for preapproved offers of credit.

2. **Mail the list brokers.** These are the companies that sell mailing lists to business and organizations.

You need to write to them and tell them to take you off all mailing and telemarketing lists. Some of the largest ones are:

Dunn and Bradstreet
Customer Service
899 Eaton Avenue
Bethlehem, PA 18025

Metromail Corporation List Maintenance
c/o Customer Service
901 West Bond
Lincoln, NE 68521-3694

R.L. Polk and Co.—Name Deletion File
List Compilation Development
26955 North West Highway
Southfield, MI 48034

Database America
Compilation Department
100 Paragon Drive
Montvale, NJ 07645-0419

3. Directly contact the companies that are sending you junk mail and request to be removed from their list.

Use their postage-paid postcards or enclosed envelopes, if you want to do it on their dime. Write "Refused—Return to Sender" on unopened envelopes you receive that say "address correction requested." And finally, call any catalog or junk mail's toll-free number and ask them to remove your name and address from their list.

These are somewhat time-consuming steps to take but are well worth it. Junk mail and telemarketing are not only annoying, they are a violation of your privacy. Only *you* should have a say in who has access to your private information. Com-

The SAFETY CHICK Checklist

WHAT TO DO IF YOU'RE A VICTIM OF FRAUD

IF YOUR CREDIT CARDS ARE STOLEN:

- ☑ Contact all of your credit card companies *immediately* to report stolen cards.
- ☑ Put a "fraud alert" on all accounts.
- ☑ File a report with local police.

IF YOU ARE A VICTIM OF IDENTITY THEFT:

- ☑ Get a copy of your credit report.
- ☑ File a report with the Federal Trade Commission: (877) 438-4338
- ☑ Contact the fraud department of the three major credit bureaus:
  Experian: (888) 397-3742
  Equifax: (800) 525-6285
  TransUnion: (800) 680-7289
- ☑ Contact all creditors with whom you have found evidence of fraudulent charges on bills.
- ☑ Contact all financial institutions where you have accounts.
- ☑ Contact the fraud department of the major bank verification companies:
  CheckRite: (800) 766-2748
  ChexSystems: (800) 428-9623
  CrossCheck: (800) 552-1900
  Equifax: (800) 437-5120
  TeleCheck: (800) 710-9898
- ☑ Contact the Social Security Administration: (800) 269-0271
- ☑ Contact the Internal Revenue Service: (800) 829-0433

panies that sell your information for personal gain should not be rewarded.

Become a Consumer Assertive Safety Chick. Don't be afraid to question any person asking you for sensitive information like your Social Security number or mother's maiden name. First, determine if the information is required or voluntary. If it's voluntary, decline to give out private numbers. If it's required, give out only what is necessary. Verify who is asking you for the information and how it will be used. Make it clear that you do not want your data available to third parties. If you are not satisfied with answers on how your personal information is handled, do your business elsewhere.

Chapter 6

Guys Who Won't Take *No* for an Answer

How to Protect Yourself from a Stalker

An obsessed fan was stalking tennis star Martina Hingis. He was writing her letters, professing his love to her, showing up at matches demanding to see her. She wisely obtained a restraining order. (Smart move. Remember what happened to Monica Seles?) Over the course of the following week, I was appalled to hear male television and radio reporters sympathizing with the stalker— "Was he really trying to hurt her, or just a love-struck fan?"—as well as speculating that the stalking laws have gone too far.

I cannot tell you how many times I have heard the argument from men over the years, "Jeez, all the guy was trying to do was ask the girl out. You know how girls say 'no' when they really mean 'yes'?" or "If I had taken 'no' for an answer, my wife and I wouldn't be married today!" When we were first trying to get the anti-stalking law passed in every state, I went on several television and radio shows. I always met the same argument, either from defense attorneys, ACLU members or just men in general. None of them seemed to get the fact that the crime of stalking was a whole lot more than an innocent guy trying to woo a girl into courtship. Most people identify the crime of stalking with celebrities. Madonna, Steven Spielberg, and Gwyneth Paltrow all have been victims, but the truth is that stalking is a crime that can touch anyone.

"Every step you take— every move you make—I'll be watching you."
—Sting, the lyrics of "Every Breath You Take"

While women are the primary targets, men can be victims as well. A recent study conducted by the Department of Justice reported that 1 in 12 women and 1 in 45 men would be stalked at least once in their lives. The victims are usually between 19 and 39 years of age. Each year, more than 1 million women and 370,000 men become victims of stalking. Men are the primary perpetrators.

A stalker is defined by the California Penal Code as "any person who willfully, maliciously and repeatedly follows or harasses another person and who makes a credible threat with the intent to place that person in reasonable fear for his or her safety." To find a definition of the stalking law in your state, check with your attorney general's office or refer to the Resource Guide at the end of the book. The bottom line is, if a person makes another person feel uncomfortable or fearful, the behavior is unacceptable and needs to be stopped.

We have come a long way legally since the crime of stalking was given a name. Unfortunately, many people in the general population still have a difficult time recognizing that this dangerous and harassing criminal act is serious. I know it took me a while to realize that my situation was threatening. Women are so used to men making unwanted advances, we have gotten numb to their annoying persistence. Therefore, a woman might find herself the focus of an unwanted pursuer. I kept thinking that the man who was stalking me was going to stop. After he was arrested with a semi-automatic weapon and told the police he wanted to kidnap me, I came to the conclusion that this was more than a little crush. Do not let denial replace good common sense. Recognizing early signals that someone is stalking you can be the key to nipping potential danger in the bud.

A great way to combat uncertainty is with wisdom. Learning more about the crime of stalking is a great way to combat the fear of being stalked. I was fortunate enough to learn from the best. I have been the guest speaker at the yearly conference for professionals in the threat assessment field and have done numerous training workshops with these true experts. Over the years I have worked closely with retired police lieutenant John Lane, who headed up the country's first Threat Management Unit within the Los Angeles Police Department and founded the Association of Threat Assessment Professionals (ATAP). He now has his own private security company, the Omega Group. John, along with Dr. Michael Zona, one of the leading forensic psychologists on stalking; and Michael Eubanks, one of the founding members of ATAP, are some of the most experienced professionals in the field of stalking prevention. (You can pay me later, guys.) With this knowledge and through my own personal experience I feel comfortable talking freely and with a little bit of humor about this very serious subject.

Stalker Types: What Flavor Is He?

Many forensic psychologists believe there are different characteristics which define stalkers. Understanding these various types can help you assess your situation better.

There are four psychological definitions of stalkers. Unfortunately, stalkers are human, which means that even if you are able to classify a stalker, the strategic approach you might take will always be different. Now, I mean no disrespect to my forensic psychologist friends, but in addition to the clinical definitions, I have come up with some whimsical labels to help my fellow laypeople better understand these menacing deviants.

Vanilla (Simple Obsessional)

The stalker, usually male, knows the victim personally. For example: ex-lover, ex-spouse, or former employee. Like vanilla is a common ice cream flavor, Simple Obsessional is one of the most common types of stalkers. Most of these situations are related to domestic or workplace violence.

Strawberry (Love Obsessional)

The stalker is a stranger or casual acquaintance who becomes obsessed with the victim. A Love Obsessional is a little less common than a Simple Obsessional stalker, but still very familiar as stalking cases go; think of strawberry as the "love" part and, as an ice cream flavor, a close relation to vanilla.

Banana Nut (Erotomania)

The stalker, frequently female, falsely believes that the victim, usually someone famous or rich, is in love with her: Brad Pitt, Madonna, David Letterman. I believe the ice cream flavor speaks for itself.

Tutti Frutti (False Vicitmization Syndrome)

This is a conscious or unconscious desire to be placed in the role of a victim. In other words: pretending you are being stalked. This often is a woman who is trying to gain the attention of her ex, or a disturbed individual who sees this tactic as a way of getting noticed. Think of the phrase "Tutti has gone frutti" to help you remember this one.

In most cases, you would be dealing with either a Simple Obsessional or Love Obsessional stalker. All that means is that you either know the person or you don't. It doesn't make the situation better or worse. Understanding who the stalker is and why he is stalking you is the first step in "licking" the situation (to pursue the ice cream metaphor) and stopping the stalker "cold."

"Can't This Guy Take a Hint? I'm Not Interested!"

How to recognize stalking behavior

How can you tell if you are being stalked or you're just a victim of a guy who is a little slow getting the message? I believe the first step is to once again think about how you know the person. I will examine these different kinds of relationships; it is up to you to apply them to your own life and use your intuition to assess your personal situation.

The Acquaintance
Boy, do I understand this one. Let's say that you went to high school with a guy. He was on the track team with you, but you really didn't socialize with him. You never said more than "hi" when you passed him in the hallway. Years later, he tracks you down and wants to start a relationship with you. After you politely decline, he persists by repeatedly calling you, following you around town and showing up at your door with semi-automatic

weapons. Wait a minute, that's me! Anyway, you get the idea. Whether he was a former classmate or someone you run into every week at the dry cleaner, he wants a relationship with you—whether you're interested or not.

A lot of times these stalkers will misconstrue what you are telling them and twist it to mean that you are interested. For example, the guy at the dry cleaner is there every Tuesday morning when you drop off your cleaning. Finally he gets up the guts to ask you out. You tell him, "Thank you, but I'm married." What he hears in his delusional mind is: "Gee, I would really like to go out with you, but I've got this darned husband at home. Maybe we can work something out." He now begins a relentless campaign to get you to go out with him. This can include following you around town, parking in front of your house to observe you, or making harassing phone calls. It can escalate into more violent behavior. Later in the chapter, I will discuss preventive measures to take before this happens as well as ways to protect yourself from this kind of predator. This stalker would probably be of the "strawberry" flavor, although he could fall into the "banana nut" category as well.

The Nightmare Date from Hell

Let's be honest, we've all had a few of these. Your friend has a friend whose brother's roommate has a cousin who would be perfect for you. You meet him for dinner. Somewhere between the appetizer and dessert, you realize his elevator doesn't quite go to the top. You make it to the end of the night when he says, "Gee, I had a wonderful time, when can we get together again?" You, being the polite, courteous woman that you were groomed to be, lie and say, "Well, thank you, but I'm swamped with work right now; I'll have to let you know." Then you spend the next week screening your calls.

In most cases the guy will get the hint. Unfortunately, it can also be the precise catalyst that prompts a stalker. Suddenly you start receiving unwanted flowers or gifts from the guy. He starts showing up at your work. It can escalate to threatening phone calls, damage to your personal property, or worse. This stalker is also of the "strawberry" variety, but could also be classified as "plain vanilla."

The "Ex"

In the immortal words of Neil Sadaka, "Breaking up is hard to do," especially if you are not the one initiating the breakup. In many countries, it is absolutely unacceptable for the woman to leave the man. Doing so can lead to death. In America, the land of many cultures, some men have difficulty dealing with separation or divorce. Rejection is not an option they accept, and it can lead to intense harassment or physical violence. Protecting yourself from these types of stalkers can be especially difficult when you share joint custody of your kids. I talk about this more in chapter 9.

Obviously, identifying potential warning signs before something happens can enhance your chances of staying safe. For example, you are divorced and have met a new man. Your ex-husband is extremely angry and starts making threatening phone calls to both you and your new boyfriend. He starts showing up in front of your house at all hours of the night. This is unusual behavior for him; he was not abusive toward you when you were married. But you never know what is going to trigger stalking behavior. Depression, drug use, or extreme stress all can be contributing factors. Whatever the reason might be, there is *no excuse* for the behavior. "Vanilla" is definitely his flavor.

The Co-Worker

This can be similar to the acquaintance scenario, but the difference is that you see this co-worker every day. He could be the guy in the snack lounge or the mail room. He has eyes for you, but you don't even notice him. The problem comes when he starts making unwanted advances. Because you work in the same building, you can't get away from him. He might start leaving notes on your desk or sending unwanted e-mails. He may even become more aggressive in front of co-workers. For example, you already have rejected his e-mail inviting you to dinner days before. He approaches you in line at the cafeteria and loudly says, "Why haven't you returned any of my phone calls? I really thought we had something going here!" which in and of itself is bizarre, considering you have never even had a conversation with this person. This guy would probably be classified as a "strawberry," but could be considered a "banana nut" if he were under the delusion that you were in love with him.

Another type of stalker in the workplace is a disgruntled employee or client. I go into further detail about this in Chapter 7, Working Girl, but for now, let me give you a couple of examples. You are a sales manager. One of your employees is performing poorly. He frequently is late for work, is not meeting his quota, and has a negative attitude. You pull him aside and explain that if his work does not improve, you will have to let him go. He becomes angry and begins to threaten you. He storms out of your office and begins a campaign of harassment towards you and your family.

Once again, "vanilla" is the flavor choice.

The Cyborg

The computer has become an increasingly popular tool of harassment among stalkers. Many victims find themselves being bombarded by e-mails or computer viruses, or having their personal information spread all over the Internet by a cowardly harasser. Because of the vastness of the system, anonymity is quite easy to obtain. Thanks to federal anti-stalking laws, task forces have popped up all over the country designed to combat this obnoxious and threatening behavior. For more information on cyberstalking and using the Internet safely, see chapter 8, CyberGirl. This computer geek can fall into almost any of the "flavors."

Me, Myself, and I
There also is a strange phenomenon of people who stalk themselves. This usually is a person who is trying to win back an ex-lover by pretending they are in danger, or someone who is extremely insecure and is falsely claiming they are being stalked to gain attention. Either way, a secure Safety Chick would never fall prey to this "tutti frutti" stupidity.

All of these are examples of stalking behavior. I hope you are never a recipient of this unwanted attention, but if you or someone you know is, please do something about it.

Enough Is Enough
What to do if you are being stalked

Each stalking case is different yet similar. What I mean is that there are certain procedures that you would follow in every stalking case and some strategic actions you would not. For example, the first thing that every victim should do in every stalking case is to make it clear to the stalker that she wants nothing to do with him. Something that can be different in every stalking case is whether you should obtain a restraining order or not. Let me go through a list of things to do when dealing with a stalker and explain in more detail the reasons for each. (At the end of this chapter there is an anti-stalking Safety Chick Checklist that you can refer to.)

Remember: The key to staying alive as a stalking victim is to stay one step ahead of your stalker.

1. **The first moment your intuition tells you that the person's behavior is inappropriate, you should tell the stalker loud and clear, "I want no further contact with you of any kind."** Even if he does not comply, you can tell the police that you have made your feelings clear to the stalker. Now his behavior can be considered harassment.

2. **Avoid any further contact with the stalker.** Sometimes this can be quite difficult. It might mean that you have to shop somewhere else, find new restaurants, even change your address. Many victims believe that they should not have to turn their lives upside down because of a stalker. I wholeheartedly agree, but until they can put all stalkers on an iceberg somewhere in the middle of Antarctica, your safety is more important than where you buy your groceries. This also means never, ever communicating with a stalker in person, on the phone, by e-mail or snail mail. Any contact, even if you're screaming a stream of obscenities, can be interpreted by the stalker as a sign of encouragement.

3. **Document all incidents.** Get a journal and write down the time, date, and a description of every incident. Whether it's a phone call or a sighting of the suspect parked in front of your home, make a note of it. Even if you don't think it's important, the police do. In order to charge a suspect with the crime of stalking, you need to show a laundry list of harassing behavior. Every little bit helps.

At the end of this chapter, on page 110, I've included a sample Stalking Incident Log that tells you the kind of information you should try to gather when documenting a stalking incident.

4. Notify the police. If the stalker persists after you have made it clear that you want no further contact, notify the police. It is best to visit to the police station and sit down with an officer to make the report, rather than having a police officer and patrol car come to your home, which can be conspicuous if you want to keep your case private. Be clear and calm. Bring all evidence and documentation with you. The police are there to help you, but you are the one who needs to facilitate your case. You need to work with the police in getting the stalker to stop his/her threatening behavior. That means following the list of actions in this chapter as well as all instructions given to you by your police department.

As I said earlier, we have come a long way legally since the crime of stalking was given a name. While there are laws in every state, some police departments remain relatively mystified by the behavior. That's why it is so important for you to be a reliable and organized "client." If you still are not getting a good response from your local police, contact one of the victim's rights organizations listed on pages 207–8.

5. Save all evidence. This means that ugly teddy bear that he left on your doorstep, the dead flowers he left on your desk, even the stupid Post-it note he left on your car. Make sure you save any telephone messages on your answering machine or voice mail as well. All of this is extremely helpful to the police and aids in the prosecution of your stalker.

6. Keep a camera and/or video camera with you. Snap his picture (a Polaroid is easiest) or videotape his antics on film. Remember, it's your word against his. The more concrete evidence, the better. This *does not* mean that you should put yourself in danger just to get the shot. Use your common sense.

7. **Keep an emergency contact list.** Make sure you have an easily accessible list in your purse or glove compartment, or on your refrigerator door, of names and numbers that could be critical in your time of need. For example: the police officer or detective who has been assigned to your case, your attorney or prosecutor, and any neighbors or family who can assist you. And of course, don't forget 911.

8. **Notify family, friends, neighbors, and co-workers that you are being stalked.** For a lot of victims, this can be uncomfortable or embarrassing, but your personal well-being should outweigh any awkwardness. If you have a picture of your stalker, make copies for your *trusted* friends, family, neighbors, and co-workers. If you know the suspect's name, vehicle description, and work and home addresses, distribute that information as well. Your neighbors can be your eyes and ears when you are not home, your co-workers can ward off any unexpected visits from the stalker by stopping him at the door before he gets to you, and your family is an essential support group for you in an incredibly stressful and emotional time. Also make sure that your children are escorted safely to and from school. Notify school officials of your situation and make it clear that only authorized family members and friends are to pick up or drop off your kids.

9. **Obtain a restraining order.** This is a legal document from the court which restricts the stalker from contacting you or coming near you in any way. Violators are subject to arrest. This is a first step in getting your tormentor prosecuted for the crime of stalking.

But a restraining order is not always the answer. Sometimes, mostly in cases of domestic violence, this can be a catalyst to violence for the stalker. Even a simple piece of paper restricting the stalker from getting near his victim can provoke retaliation. Another problem with a restraining order is that the victim must list the various locations prohibited to the stalker—which doesn't make any sense if the victim has just relocated and is in hiding. Filing a restraining order is something that should be discussed with the police officer or detective that has been assigned to your case. Bottom line: Proceed with caution.

10. **Believe in yourself.** Being stalked is traumatic. Many victims feel that they have done something to make the stalker behave this way. Remember: It is not your fault! Everyone in this world is responsible for their own actions. The prototypical stalker is emotionally weak and disturbed. You have done nothing to provoke this violating, destructive behavior. Stay strong, Chick!

Incognito

Keeping your personal information private

Stalkers aside, every person should take certain security measures to keep personal information private. Remember that you are the ruler of your private information. Don't be bullied by companies wanting to put you on a mailing list, or a store clerk demanding your home address. Nobody, but nobody, is entitled to that information unless *you* say so. Consistency on this point allows you to stay incognito from unwanted pursuers. Only *you* decide who gets to know the location of "your own private Idaho."

Telephone

1. **Request an unlisted telephone number.** That way, *you* decide who has your number. It also cuts down on all those obnoxious telemarketers.

2. **Never give your full name when signing up for service.** Just give your initial and last name, or—if possible—a different name completely. For example: T. Bono or T-Bone Enterprises.

3. **Avoid giving out your home number to anyone except friends, family, and school/child care providers.** If you are having your car serviced or you need to give a number to a store clerk, always provide a cell phone or work number. You never can be sure what these people will do with your number. If they enter it in their data base, the next thing you know, your private number is on every telemarketing list in town. Then there is a much greater possibility of your personal information falling into the wrong hands.

4. **Do not list your home number in a directory of any kind.** Always use your cell phone or work number if you want to be listed in a church or school directory. People will still be able to reach you. Remember, if they are your friends, they already have your number.

Mail

1. **Get a P.O. box.** You can go to the nearest post office or private mail center, for example, Mail Boxes Etc. and sign up. The difference between the post office and a private

mail center is that at the post office they assign you a post office box number, and they do not accept UPS or FedEx packages. Private mail centers give you an actual address and will accept packages. This is a bit more expensive than the post office, but might be worth it if you get a lot of parcels in the mail. Only give out your home address to friends and family. This not only cuts down on junk mail, it gives you a post office box number or address to list on your checks, drivers license, and other forms that circulate through the public sector.

2. **Don't advertise your name on your mailbox.** This includes apartments and condominiums. Anyone who comes to your door should already know your name and apartment/condo number. If they don't, they shouldn't be there.

3. **Avoid receiving packages at your home.** All packages should be sent to your post office box. An inconvenience? Maybe. But compare the hassle of picking up a package at the post office to a stranger showing up at your door uninvited.

Rebecca Schaeffer, the actress from the popular 1980s TV sitcom *My Sister Sam* was killed by her stalker on the front steps of her apartment building. She had her name listed right on the intercom system outside the building. The man, who is serving life in prison for her murder, buzzed her apartment, which summoned her downstairs and into his waiting bullet.

Bills/Credit Cards/Checks

1. **Do not have any of your bills sent to your home.** Always list your post office box as your mailing address. An even better solution is to pay your bills online—but do it safely. Companies like Paytrust or E-bills are great solutions for paying your bills securely and on time. If you have a personal accountant, discuss the possibility of setting up a system to have your bills sent to and paid by them.

2. **Do not list your full name on your utilities, credit cards, or personal checks.** Always use your first initial and last name for bills and credit cards. If possible, use a company name or trust. Use an initial and last name or company name on your checks, and make sure to use your post office box or accountant's address. There is no need to put personal numbers like telephone, driver's license, social security, or any other private piece of information on your check. Think about how many people come into contact with that check before it gets to the bank.

3. **Do not list private contact information on credit card or utility applications.** Once again, your address should be your post offic box, your bill paying service, or your accountant. The phone number should be your cell phone or work listing.

4. **Do not fill out random credit card applications that you get in the mail.** If you want a credit card, go to your bank or call a company directly. Filling out forms that require extremely personal information such as Social Security and bank account numbers should be done in a secure environment with a bank clerk or account manager.

For more information on credit cards and checking account safety, refer to chapter 5, A Girl's Gotta Shop.

Owning Property

1. **Do not list property in your name.** This is extremely important when buying a personal residence. When holding title, make sure you don't use your name. Again, try to use a company or trust. At least use initials. The title document goes straight to the county hall of records and is available to the public, which means that anyone has access to this personal information. Some companies will hold title on your property securely for a monthly fee (for example, The Chicago Trust Company of California), which means that they are listed on the Deed of Trust and other records regarding the property. This is an effective way to foil a stalker trying to track you down by searching county records.

2. **Keep your name and address out of the real estate company's data base.** Make it clear to the real estate agent who sold you the property that it is vital that they keep you off their mailing list. Once an agent writes up a sales contract, that information goes through the company. You don't want to end up on hundreds of mailing lists after you spent the time and money to keep your records private.

The Department of Motor Vehicles

Make sure your post office box, not your home address, is listed on your driver's license. Recent laws have been passed restricting personal information that can be given out by the Department of Motor Vehicles (DMV). In the past, almost anyone could find out a person's address, telephone number, and other personal information from the DMV. Now, it is illegal to give out personal information to unauthorized individuals. Ask for a "Request for Privacy of Personal Information" form when you apply for your license; this is available in most states under the Driver Privacy Act. Better safe than sorry: Don't give out your address.

Registering to Vote

Be careful when you are registering. A voter registration card is also public record. Therefore, you need to be careful about the information you put down. You can request confidential voter status on your application or, depending on where you live, you may be able to use your post office box. If you have further questions or issues regarding your voter information, contact the registrar's office in your county or state.

Catalogs, Magazine Subscriptions, and Internet Shopping

Do not have shopping items shipped to your home address. I know this is a tough one. No one loves catalog shopping more than I do. But you must receive your mail order purchases at a post office box or, if it's permissible, your office. Once you give a catalog company or a magazine subscription or an Internet Web site your home address, consider yourself on every mailing list in the Western Hemisphere!

Do not give personal information over the phone or Internet. Always use your cell or work number and your P.O.

box for your mailing address. The key to keeping your personal information private is consistency. Once you get your mailing address, cell phone, and bill-paying system together, stick to the plan. Never deviate from your system. That way, if you do receive a phone call or mail from an unauthorized source, it is easier to track down and correct the problem.

Don Your Camouflage Gear

Be your own special ops agent

There is nothing more debilitating than living like a hunted animal. If you find yourself in this weakened state, get your power back! Take control. I am not suggesting that you turn into Rambo and hunt your stalker down. What I am suggesting is to that you take steps to decrease the chance of falling victim to your stalker. Here are some extra Safety Chick tips for the heat of battle.

Your Antennae Should Be Way, Way Up!
When you leave or return to your home, take the time to drive up and down the streets for about a four-block radius. Scan every parked car for the stalker's vehicle. I cannot tell you how many times this saved me from walking into my stalker's trap. Several times I saw his car parked down the street. Instead of going home, I would drive straight to the police station and make a report. If you see the car, do not approach it. Drive straight to the police station for help.

Curb Appeal

Stand on the front porch of your home or entryway to your apartment. Look across the street, down the block, and around the corner. Where could a car park or a person stand and watch your comings and goings? Once you have determined these locations, always scan the area when exiting or entering your home to make sure the stalker is not watching you from one of those positions. Make sure there are no obstacles blocking the front of your house from the street. If the police are driving by, they must be able to see your front door clearly. This is not paranoid behavior. This is a Safety Chick getting in touch with her surroundings.

Sensory Perception

Install sensor lights all around your house. Nothing bursts an intruder's bubble more than a bright light exploding through the cloak of darkness. Also, install an alarm system which will notify you if an intruder is trying to enter your home. (See chapter 4, Beauty Night, for tips on how to feel safe in your own home.)

Don't Panic, Get a Button

If you have filed a police report and are a victim of a stalker, check with your local victim services office: Many security companies provide victims with a necklace-type panic button. When pressed, it calls the local police department directly for immediate help.

Set a Trap

Check with your local Victim Services office and immediately have a "trap" set on your phone. Most phone companies provide this free service to victims of harassing phone calls or a stalker (if you have filed a report with the police department). They will install a device on your phone that keeps a record of who called you and when, even if the number is unlisted. Check to see if this service is offered in your community.

Miss Confidentiality

Most states offer the address confidentiality program (ACP) through their attorney general's office. If you are a victim of a stalker, domestic violence, or sexual assault, you can designate the attorney general's office as your legal agent for the service of processing legal documents and receiving mail. In return you will be assigned a substitute address that has no relation to your home, work, or school address. Check with your state attorney general's office for more information on ACP.

If It Feels Right, Do It

The feeling of being stalked is a very personal thing. Every victim is different; therefore, therapeutic measures will be different. If you want to learn how to use a gun, do it; just make sure a professional trains you, and register your gun legally. If you want to take self-defense classes, do it; I highly recommend this as it helps work out any pent-up frustration you might be feeling. If you want to talk to a therapist, the clergy, or another professional, do it. You should do whatever makes you feel comfortable and empowered.

Be Resourceful

The crime of stalking is one of the most devastating offenses a victim can experience. Since 1997, we have an anti-stalking law in every state and a national law that protects victims as well. Law enforcement agencies all over the country have taken the Los Angeles Police Department's lead and created anti-stalking departments within their divisions. If you are a victim, there are several places you can go for help. The first is your local police station. There are also wonderful victims' rights organizations that can provide further assistance. Look in the Resource Guide at the end of the book.

L.A. Law

If you find yourself in court dealing with your stalker, that is somewhat good news, although you're not home free. That means that he has been arrested or detained. Now it's up to the legal system to help you. A lot of district attorney's offices now have anti-stalking departments within their divisions, thanks to the Los Angeles District Attorney's office and assistant District Attorney Rhonda Saunders. She has prosecuted high-profile stalking cases involving Madonna, Steven Spielberg, and Michael J. Fox. Not only is she an extremely competent and ferocious prosecutor, but she's definitely a sassy, strong Safety Chick as well. Rhonda is one of the first women pioneers in the anti-stalking field. She travels around the country teaching prosecutors and other law enforcement professionals the ins and outs of stalking laws and other legislation related to stalking. You would be extremely lucky to have her, or someone like her, prosecuting your stalker.

In My Expert Opinion

I must be honest and tell you that writing this chapter brings back a lot of raw emotion from my stalking ordeal. It is because of that emotion that I am able to write this book with such strong conviction. I am extremely proud of the progress our judicial system has made in prosecuting these manipulative predators—which isn't to say that there isn't room for improvement, such as stronger sentencing for offenders. The most constructive thing about the creation of the anti-stalking laws is that they actually stop violence before it escalates.

Implementing the proper procedures allows police to arrest a criminal before he/she does physical harm to his/her victim. This is the first time a law can actually prevent a rape or murder from happening. My hat goes off to U.S. Congressman Ed Royce, who supported this law from the very beginning. On behalf of Safety Chicks everywhere, thank you!

The SAFETY CHICK Checklist
WHAT TO DO IF YOU ARE BEING STALKED

☑ Make it clear to the stalker you want no further contact.

☑ Document all incidents in a journal—include the time, date, and description of the event. (See the Incident Log and Incident Report on page 110.)

☑ Save all evidence—telephone messages, e-mails, letters, gifts, etc.

☑ Contact the police—take all evidence to the police station.

☑ Keep a camera and/or video camera on hand—snap his picture or videotape his antics. DO NOT put yourself in danger to get the shot. Stay in your car or home when taking the picture and make sure the environment is safe before you videotape any damage that has been done.

☑ Make an emergency contact list for you and your family—include telephone numbers of police station (dial 911 if it's urgent), name and badge number of officer assigned to your case, child care or school contact numbers, and the name and number of your attorney or prosecutor.

☑ Avoid any further contact with the stalker—DO NOT communicate with your stalker in any way. Change your daily routine. Shop at a different grocery store; drive home a different way every day. If your situation is extremely dangerous, relocate. (Talk with police officials or victim assistance organizations for help.)

THE SAFETY CHICK
STALKING INCIDENT LOG

Your name/contact number: _____

Description of suspect: _____

Name: _____

Sex: _____

Race: _____

Date of birth: _____

Height/weight: _____

Eyes/hair color: _____

Home address/phone number: _____

Work address/phone number: _____

Vehicle description (Make, model, color, license plate number):

_____

THE SAFETY CHICK INCIDENT REPORT

Date: _____

Time: _____

Location: _____

Description of incident/evidence collected: _____

_____

_____

Names and phone numbers of witnesses: _____

_____

_____

Police Report # and name/badge # of reporting officer: _____

_____

_____

(You may make several copies of this form and use it for your records)

Chapter 7

Working Girl

Tips on Recognizing and Avoiding Workplace Violence

The public's perception of workplace violence is a disgruntled employee storming into an office and shooting co-workers. Even though that scenario only makes up about 5 percent of all criminal incidents in the workplace, it is still something with which Americans are extremely concerned. Great strides have been made in the past few years to put procedures in place which aid in deterring workplace violence.

One of the most volatile departments for any company is the human resources department. This is where most people are hired and fired, which guarantees an emotional environment. A good friend of mine worked in the human resources department of a large, high-end hotel chain. She told me about two of her co-workers who had fired a man working at one of the hotels. His job performance had been lacking and he had many problems with other employees. He had a history of aggressive behavior and was a perfect candidate for post-termination violence, yet no one put any special security measures in place. Three days after being let go, he returned to the company, was

111

admitted through the security checkpoint without his I.D. badge (he said he had left it at his desk), and made straight for the human resources department. He took the two female supervisors who had fired him into an office, locked the door, and raped both of them at gunpoint. When he was finished, he calmly walked out of the office through security and out the front door.

The most important lesson from this tragic incident is that every company *absolutely* needs to have security measures in place that help protect employees from becoming victims of workplace violence. This chapter enlightens working Americans to various occupational hazards and gives fundamental information on procedures to take back to their office.

Whether you're a business executive, department store clerk, or bus driver, there are potential dangers in any workplace environment. Even though we think of "going postal" as a whole lot more than going to the post office to mail a letter, the reality is that workplace violence is not just the result of disgruntled employees bent on revenge. Current crime statistics show that workplace violence is clustered in certain occupational settings, and the most common violence is robbery-related, not the result of an unbalanced employee. Still, the rage of an emotionally disturbed employee is something that every working American has thought about. This chapter offers some perspective on this highly publicized crime.

Incidents of workplace violence have more to do with the job itself than the person performing the job. Recent statistics from the U.S. Department of Labor Occupational Safety and Health Administration (OSHA) show that jobs dealing with public contact, the exchange of money, delivery of service and goods, health care, and community service are those with the highest safety risk. It almost makes you want to respond to that "work at home—get rich quick" junk mail scheme. (But don't.)

Risky Business

Is your occupation one of the risky ones?

As I mentioned above, occupations with the greatest risk of workplace violence generally deal with the exchange of money (for example, convenience store clerk, cab driver) or public security (for example, police officer or security guard). The occupations that have the greatest amount of nonfatal workplace assaults are nursing home attendants, social workers, and hospital workers. There are other professions that might not be so obvious. Recognizing occupations that have potential hazards helps employees develop safety measures and heightens their awareness of personal safety.

Thank Heaven for 7-11?

Late-night store clerk or taxi driver probably are not the best career choices for a woman, but there are safety measures you can take to protect yourself in any profession. For example, if you work in a convenience store, make sure that all cash is put in a locked dropped box safe to which you have no access. Signs should be clearly posted alerting the public to that fact. A bullet-resistant barrier between you and the customer is an added piece of protection. The best safety measure, however, is not to work late-night shifts. It is common knowledge that the graveyard shift has the highest incidence of crime.

Florence Nightingales Beware

Nurses or attendants in a nursing home or hospital are high among workplace assault victims. The patients they're dealing with guarantee that. Many hospital attendants handle mentally ill patients who are violent or patients in a temporary agitated state, thus putting themselves in continuous jeopardy.

According to the U.S. Department of Labor, Occupational Safety, and Health Administration, some 2 million American workers are victims of workplace violence each year.

Holding Court

Working within a judicial system can also be a volatile profession. The stakes can be high in a criminal, family, small claims, *or* jury trial. Those working within the system can become targets of aggression by a defendant, a disappointed litigant, or persons close to them.

Vote for Me

Holding public office is a commendable profession. It can also be extremely dangerous. Politicians make decisions that affect many people, leaving them open to criticism and retaliation by extremists with opposing views.

Permit Me

Employees who work in permit or licensing offices can be the targets of threats or assaults. Anxious people who don't get what they want—a permit to build some monstrosity in their backyard, for example—can become violent and turn their aggressions toward the bearer of the bad news.

Finally, in order to recognize persons who might become violent, you need to understand the definition of workplace violence.

Cubicle Wars

How to identify co-workers who might be candidates for violence

In California, the San Mateo County Prevention of Workplace Violence program was designed and developed by Sarita M. Ledet, M.F.T. It was introduced to government employees at the South San Francisco Workplace Violence Conference 2001 by Sergeant Marc Dowdy of the San Mateo County Sheriff's Department. Sergeant Dowdy's insight and material contributed greatly to this chapter.

The definition of "workplace violence" comes from three sources:

1. **The media.** Television stations, newspapers, etc., have defined workplace violence as an armed disgruntled employee or client who storms into an office and randomly or selectively shoot other employees. (Workplace Violence Institute)

2. **The F.B.I.** Any act that may threaten the safety and/or property at the worksite.

3. **American Federation of State, County, and Municipal Employees (AFSCME).** The workplace is defined as any place a worker performs a job. Workplace violence is defined as any act of aggression that causes physical or emotional harm.

Combining these three definitions provides a comprehensive description of violence in the workplace. But just what type of behavior constitutes workplace violence? According to the San Mateo County policy there are three categories.

1. **Acts of violence.** The exertion of force or aggression with the intent of causing injury or abuse.

2. **Threats of violence.** Remarks, gestures, or communication that cause an individual to be concerned about personal safety or the safety of others.

3. **Domestic violence.** Abuse committed to a spouse or former spouse, cohabitant or former cohabitant, current or past dating relationship, or person with whom the victim had a child.

Workplace violence can come in many forms. Two of the most obvious are physical aggression: hitting, kicking, grabbing, blocking movement, slapping, or pushing; and threatening communication: e-mail, snail mail, verbal, in person or over the telephone, faxes, gestures, or drawings. Some not so obvious would be bringing unauthorized weapons to the workplace, or a disgruntled customer who repeatedly files lawsuits against a company and is hostile toward the employees. Violent behavior is easy to spot when it's happening; the idea is to learn how to recognize the signs before the violence actually occurs.

An Inside Job

Violence at the workplace can be from external or internal sources. For example, an external source would be a person who has no legitimate reason to be at the workplace, or someone who may have a reason to be at the workplace but is not an employee. An internal source would be a current employee, contractor, or consultant or a former employee, contractor, or consultant.

Who Could It Be?

An employee or outsider who exhibits certain types of behavior can be classified with the potential for violent behavior. Use your intuition, and tap into the behavioral signs that can indicate impending danger. Potentially violent individuals can possess some of these general characteristics:

○ **Inflexible and chronically disgruntled**
○ **Suffer from paranoid disorders**
○ **Cause trouble on the job**
○ **Are quick to perceive unfairness or malice in others**
○ **Refuse to take responsibility for problems**

○ **Often challenge management requests, passively or actively**

○ **Change jobs frequently**

○ **Have a deep sense of entitlement**

○ **Have a past history of violent acts**

Other personal factors that might contribute to the risk of violent behavior include physical or mental health problems, relationship problems with partner or spouse, abuse of drugs or alcohol, or stress as the primary caretaker of the family.

White Collar Crime

Frequently, those who already are committing crimes are those who commit workplace violence. For example, an employee stealing data or tampering with records is already dealing with high stress. Fear of imminent exposure could trigger desperate actions.

"Good hours, excellent pay, fun place to work, paid training, mean boss. Oh well, four out of five isn't bad."

—Help-wanted ad, Palo Alto, California, newspaper

Recognizing the kind of employee or client who might commit workplace violence is one thing, but knowing how to deal with him or her is another. Most government agencies and large companies have solid policies and procedures in place to help their employees avoid workplace violence.

Proceed with Caution

You must be able to rely on management to handle volatile situations, so take the time to inquire about your company's policies and understand how to implement them. If you do not trust your supervisor or you are not comfortable with your company's procedures, talk to someone in the human resources department or a department head. You do not want to be left hanging out to dry when you make the decision to report an un-balanced co-worker.

Checking the Records

Employers should thoroughly check the backgrounds of all po-tential employees, including criminal and educational records. Gaps in their employment history should be questioned. All ref-erences listed on applications should be investigated to make sure they have no criminal record and that the information they pro-vided is accurate. This is the first and best way to weed out pos-sible problem employees.

Did You Get the Memo?

Policies and procedures to implement at your workplace

It might seem scary or embarrassing to report the problem be-havior of a co-worker. When we were children we were condi-tioned to believe that reporting another child's bad behavior to an authoritative figure meant that we were "tattletales" and would be ostracized by our peers. If we did report someone, we were afraid they would find out and retaliate against us. In order to get out of that mindset, you must realize that *not* re-porting problem behavior directly affects you in more ways than one.

Not reporting the problem because you are afraid that the un-balanced co-worker will retaliate is understandable, but most companies have strict confidentiality policies that all employees are legally bound to maintain. Plus, going to work every day dreading interaction with the co-worker, walking on eggshells, or going out of your way to avoid being around the person is living in fear, which no hip Chick should tolerate.

Path to Violence

One of the many pieces of valuable information that stuck in my mind after a seminar on school shootings presented by Secret Service agent Dr. Robert Fein was his idea that there is usually a "path to murder." Rarely does someone spontaneously show up at a school or workplace and start shooting. After the fact, many people realize that they subconsciously or consciously knew that the event was going to take place; they knew the person was leading up to a horrific event and did nothing about it.

You Make the Call

For example, let's say a co-worker is despondent at work. His job performance has slowed and his demeanor is unusually depressed and angry. You have known this employee for years, and in the past, he has been happy and productive. There are two possible ways you could handle the situation, and how you handle the situation could make a huge difference in the outcome. You could ignore your co-worker's behavior and let him become more and more depressed and angry, which could result in a show of violence. Or you could talk to your supervisor or boss about your co-worker's behavior. Explain that he was not always this depressed and angry, and he was productive in the past.

If you choose the first method, at the very least, he could be fired and a new employee would replace him. Instead of helping the old co-worker overcome the problem, you end up doubling your workload while you train a replacement. This creates extra work and stress for you. At the very worst, by not reporting your co-worker you could become a victim of workplace violence.

If you choose the second method, your supervisor would bear the responsibility of dealing with the potential problem instead of you. Your co-worker might respond more readily to a supervisor's suggestions and concerns than to yours. He also may recognize that he has a problem and get help. If he becomes defensive and uncooperative instead, the company can choose to terminate him. This might again leave you with the added work of training a new employee, but you will be safe from possible workplace violence.

The reason for presenting these scenarios is to help you recognize that it's in your best interest to be a part of preventing violence at the workplace. The reality is, an unbalanced co-worker can ultimately affect you and your job performance. The sooner you deal with the situation, the sooner the problem will be resolved. Your motivating factor for reporting possible workplace violence is simple: your well-being.

Teamwork

If you are a supervisor or manager, there should be a team within your company or business that facilitates workplace violence solutions. This team usually consists of management, human resources, unions, workers, in-house security or law enforcement, and mental health counselors. The goal of a workplace violence team is to solve problems through conflict resolution strategies. If no one in your company has been trained, see the Resource Guide for a program in your area. There are wonderful workplace violence training programs offered all over the country.

Train, Train, Train

The proper training of workers in conflict resolution approaches can reduce the risk of volatile situations escalating into physical violence. Training that addresses hazards associated with worksites or specific job tasks (for instance, repetetive motion, such as an assembly line, which leads to boredom or irritability) and prevention also should be an important part of employee education.

What Works in Preschool Can Work for You

When my oldest boy started preschool, a main goal of the school was teaching the children conflict resolution. The thought of a three-year-old turning to a classmate and saying, "You knocked down my tower of blocks and that made me sad," was hard for me to conceive. Yet over the course of eight months, I saw these children transform into little human beings who could resolve almost any altercation by themselves and without violence. My son is now eleven. I must say that he and the boys who went through the program still use those skills. It is reflected in their mature and kind personalities and their success both in and out of the classroom.

Eight-Step Conflict Resolution

Try implementing these steps the next time you have a conflict at home or at the office. For example, let's say you and your co-worker have a "temperature" issue, meaning you are always hot in your cubicle and he is always cold. Don't laugh, it's often the smallest problems that escalate into bigger issues.

Step 1. Determine the goal that you want to reach. You both want to be comfortable.

Step 2. Make a goal statement to the person you are dealing with. Calmly ask if you could either turn down the heater or turn up the air conditioner to make the work climate more comfortable.

Step 3. Listen to and try to understand the response you get. The co-worker says that he is freezing and he would like the heat turned up.

Step 4. Deal with resistance in a manner that will keep you from arguing or falling deeper into conflict. Calmly suggest that you need to work together to come to a solution.

Step 5. Define what you are willing to do to remedy the situation. Be clear and specific about what you mean. Offer to purchase a small space heater to keep below his desk, or try getting a fan for your cubicle.

Step 6. If the person does not want to comply, attempt to explain the consequences or problems that will be created by not complying. It is important to do so in a tone that is nonthreatening. Explain that it is uncomfortable and non-productive to constantly bicker about the heat and you will need to take this up with a supervisor.

Step 7. Wait, watch, and listen to the reaction.

Step 8. Implement the consequences and restate the goal if the conflict continues. Buy him a sweater and get a fan.

I have tried this on my husband about cleaning the garage . . . . Okay, so you can't eat off the garage floor, but you can finally get to the kids' bikes without breaking your neck.

Commonsense Work Safety Tips

Workplace violence teams and policies at work aid in keeping you safe, but the ultimate responsibility lies with you. Using your intuition and your Safety Chick common sense are the first steps (but you already know that). The following is a list of commonsense precautions from the BRAVE (Be Ready Against Violence Everywhere) Foundation that should be a part of every workplace. See the Resource Guide for more information.

Personal Property

○ **If you bring personal items to work, make sure they're clearly marked with your initials and employee number if you have one.**

○ **Lock your purse and other valuables in a drawer or closet at all times.**

○ **If you have your own business or you work from home, never use your private residence address or phone number in any advertisement.** Always use a cell phone or pager number.

○ **Keep your personal life private.** Don't give out social or vacation plans or details of your home life or that of your fellow co-workers to customers, other co-workers, or contracted employees.

Maintenance around the Workplace

○ **Report any lights that are flickering or not working, dimly lit corridors, any doors that don't close or lock properly, or broken windows.** Don't wait for someone else to do it.

○ **Check the identity of any stranger who asks for confidential information or any delivery or repair person who wants to enter a restricted area or remove equipment.**

○ **If you notice any suspicious person or vehicles, call security or the police.** Be especially alert outside normal working hours.

○ **Have easy-to-use phone systems installed with emergency buttons.** Security, fire, and police assistance numbers should be posted by every phone.

Entering and Exiting

○ **Be extra cautious when you are using restrooms or stairwells that are poorly lit, in isolated areas, or are open to the public.**

○ **If you plan to work late or come in early, try to arrange your schedule to work with another employee.**

○ **If you are working late, ask a security guard or co-worker to escort you to your car.**

Taking charge of your personal safety at work is a must. If your workplace doesn't have a thorough safety plan or if you are not satisfied with the procedures, express your concerns and ideas with the appropriate personnel. Besides being the Safety Chick thing to do, it can help make your place of work safe for everyone.

The SAFETY CHICK Checklist
WORKPLACE VIOLENCE POLICY

☑ Violence is *not* tolerated in the workplace.

☑ Threats against employees, visitors, customers, or vendors will *not* be tolerated.

☑ Joking or false reporting is *not* tolerated.

☑ Retaliation against employees who file a report will *not* be tolerated.

☑ All employees are responsible for making a safe environment.

☑ Employees in violation of this policy may be removed and subject to disciplinary procedures, terminated, or face criminal charges, or all of the above.

☑ The act of making a threat may in and of itself be grounds for dismissal, regardless of whether or not there was intent to carry it out.

Chapter 8

CyberGirl

Inside Tips to Help You Minimize the Dangers of Surfing the Net

Using the Internet to commit crime has become extremely prevalent in our society. I recently came across a case of cyberstalking that caught my attention for two reasons. One: The predator was an elementary school teacher; and two: He taught a course on bicycle and personal safety. (The nerve!) This creep had gotten the e-mail address of a little girl who was in one of his safety classes; he volunteered and taught such classes at several elementary schools in the area and solicited students' e-mail addresses in the course of befriending them. The little girl's mother called the sheriff's office when she intercepted an e-mail from the man that she felt was inappropriate. Over the course of a month, detectives corresponded with this sicko, masquerading as the girl. He allegedly became more and more sexually explicit before asking for a meeting and telling the victim he planned to take her to a remote location and perform various sexual acts with her. Detectives surprised him at the rendezvous spot he had set up and booked him on charges of attempted lewd and lascivious acts with a child under the age of 14.

Now that we've entered the new millennium, the information superhighway has hit mega-speed. Internet and telecommunication technologies have made extraordinary advances. Whether you live in Paris, France, or Paris, Texas, e-commerce, education, and a load of other services are made available just by the click of a mouse. With this wonderful array of accessibility also comes vulnerability. Unfortunately, what makes this technology so great also makes it a breeding ground for fraudulent scams, child sexual exploitation, and cyberstalking. The low cost, simplicity, and anonymity of use makes it easy for criminals of all types to conduct their business nearly risk-free. It is therefore up to you to "surf" smart.

As the episode on page 125 illustrates, you should monitor your child's use of the Internet and realize that corresponding with anyone on the Internet is risky business and should be done with caution and common sense.

Compute This!

Get Secure from the Inside of Your Computer Out

Before we go any further, I want to discuss basic security measures that every Internet user should follow. When I began writing this chapter, I knew about the crime of cyberstalking from law enforcement training, but I wasn't really sure how to execute all the security measures that were suggested. So I decided to find a true expert in the world of Internet security, and, boy, did I find one! John Flowers is considered to be one of the top ten Internet security experts in the cyberworld. This hacker turned dotcom founder taught the Safety Chick the ins and outs of living secure in cyberspace.

Flowers' knowledge of the Internet came from first-hand experience of hacking into various data banks and Web sites of large companies. Learning the valuable lesson as a teen that crime doesn't pay, John realized that hacking into a company's private files is easy—until you get caught. After serving time in juvenile hall, John decided to turn his "gift" into a positive contribution to the Internet community. His company, nCircle, has developed software that basically hacks into a company's computer system and finds where the system can be penetrated. Once the software identifies the weakness, the company is able to rectify the gaps before security can be compromised. In developing this software, John learned how the average Internet user is extremely vulnerable to any hacker or Internet snoop, especially one with devious intent. So it is with this knowledge that we discuss the basic security measures every cybergirl should follow.

What Is Your Computer Telling People without Your Permission?

The key to using the Internet is to try to maintain control of your personal information as well as maintain control of who has access to that information. The easiest way to start is by going into the control panel of your computer. I cannot begin to give detailed instructions on how to do this because every operating system is different. What I can tell you is to look for the Internet option setup and go from there. You are looking for the "privacy" or "security" options relating to Internet use. It is there that many security breaches can be avoided.

Cookies—Pleasing yet Dangerous

This tasty treat can also be a technical term for trouble. Picture a Web server putting a cookie jar (a software application) onto your hard drive when you log on to their site. The Web server is then able to store what is technically called a cookie: information about every move you make on their site sent from your Internet service provider (ISP) to your hard drive. They then can access that information any time they want. For the average e-commerce site, this aids in understanding and assisting the customer's needs. But, for businesses whose sole operation is to gather private information to sell to the highest bidder, your cookie can be a dangerous tool.

Cookies do serve a purpose other than using your personal information for profit. Some cookies are there to remember information you are using when on their site. For example, if you are shopping on Amazon.com and want to buy more than one item, a cookie is used to store the information from the first item you chose while you shop for the next. If you didn't use a cookie, you would have to do your shopping one item at a time—quite time-consuming for the clutch-and-grab shoppers of today. So, how can you monitor the giving out of your cookies, yet still take advantage of the conveniences that they offer?

> "Treat your password like your toothbrush. Don't let anybody else use it, and get a new one every six months."
> —Clifford Stoll

Meanwhile, Back at the Control Panel

Okay you've now located your "privacy" or "security" settings. Now look for ways you can "disable cookies," or refer to your help manual and ask, "How do I disable cookies?" The goal of this action is to find where cookies are located on your computer and tell your browser that you either do not want to accept cookies, which will limit your ability to shop or surf online, or that you want to be prompted or notified if a cookie is being placed, which gives you the opportunity to decline or accept the cookie. I have my browser set to notify me whenever an attempt is made to place a cookie on my hard drive. I have the option to say yes or no. By installing these options into your computer, you choose who gets one of your cookies, just by the click of a mouse.

Call Me Anonymous

There also is another issue in the "privacy" or "security" settings that should be addressed. It is under the "log on" feature. Again, it is impossible for me to know exactly how this looks in your system. What you want to tell your computer is to show you as "anonymous" whenever you log on to a site. Doing this is an extra security measure when surfing the net.

Remailers as Remedy

Following the two previous tips—tracking your cookie and making your "log on" anonymous, plus removing personal information, or profile, from your browser—makes you 85 percent safe on the Internet. To go the extra mile, you should sign up for a remailing service. A remailer is a means of sending and receiving e-mails anonymously. An "anonymizer" keeps people from knowing where you come from, thus making it impossible to track you down through your ISP. A great Web site for explaining this in more detail is www.andrebacard.com. Andre explains all of this in easy terms. Check the Resource Guide on page 203 for remailing Web addresses so you can decide which service is best for you.

Be Sure to Put Up Your Firewall

Firewalls are software programs or network appliances that block intruders from penetrating your internal network. This is a fabulous and easy way to protect yourself from hackers or other deviant Internet users. McAfee Personal Firewall or BlackIce PC

Protection are two solid firewall products. Any computer store can tell you more about the products and help you decide which one is best for you. They are relatively basic to install and are a must-have for Internet users. An online firewall service called zonealarm.com is a solid, reliable product to check out as well.

Now that you understand the basic security measures that you should follow, you need to understand Internet etiquette; or for you techies, netiquette. Learning the ins and outs of chatroom behavior as well as navigating around the net all plays an important role in your safety.

Scumbag@Loserville.Com

How to protect yourself from becoming a target

In 1999, former Vice President Al Gore asked then–Attorney General Janet Reno to study the growing problem of cyberstalking. In a national report, The Department of Justice came up with some interesting statistics as well as vital information that every Internet user needs to know. For example, when we previously discussed stalking, the Safety Chick reported that at least 1 in 12 women and 1 in 45 men would be stalked once in their lives. According to the Department of Justice's report, there are more than 80 million adults and 10 million children with access to the Internet. Assuming that the proportion of cyberstalking victims is even a fraction of offline stalking victims, there are potentially tens or even hundreds of thousands of victims of recent cyberstalking incidents in the United States. The Safety Chick did some investigating on her own and came up with a variety of ways that you can be victimized on the net. Whether you're technologically challenged or a full-blown computer geek, this information is important for you.

There are many similarities in the profiles and behaviors of both cyberstalkers and stalkers (see chapter 6, Guys Who Won't Take No for an Answer, to learn more about stalkers), but unlike victims of stalkers, most cyberstalking victims have a better chance of nipping the behavior in the bud. But to learn how to avert the unwanted conduct, you must first learn what constitutes cyberstalking. Many Web sites are citizen-run organizations that educate and assist victims in online privacy issues. One site in particular, www.wiredpatrol.org, is especially thorough and helpful. Run by Parry Aftab, Internet attorney and author of *The Parent's Guide to Protecting Your Children in Cyberspace*, this organization is cutting-edge in terms of Internet safety and protection.

The What, Where, Why, and How of Cyberstalking: From Wiredpatrol.org and Parry Aftab

What Is Cyberstalking?
Cyberstalking is when a person (or group) uses the Internet to stalk or harass another. This can be through e-mail, chat rooms, or any other form of electronic communication.

Where Does It Occur Most?
Most online harassment starts in the chat rooms. Because women are still the minority of the Internet population, the online chat rooms produce major competition among male users for female attention—kind of a virtual meat market/singles bar. Other sites where users can become victims are message boards and newsgroups (a virtual form of posting notes on a bulletin board) or e-mail.

Why Is Cyberstalking so Prevalent?

According to wiredpatrol.org, the anonymity of live chat can facilitate rudeness and insensitivity. The experience of real-time online communications can be similar in effect to the consumption of alcohol—a lowering of inhibitions and an increase in directness. Translation—any loser who doesn't want to leave his couch can down a six-pack (or not) and have at it.

According to wiredpatrol.org, when joining a chat room it is best to sit quietly for a few minutes to see the flow of the conversation before jumping in. This also may alert you to any people in the room you wish to avoid. If the operators of the chat forum allow people to be verbally abused and treated as sexual objects, then perhaps you should find another place to chat that has some standard of behavior.

How Are You Targeted?

Just like any other predator, cyberstalkers look for an easy target. An online stalker is someone who wants to be in control. They look for victims that are "new to the Internet"—specifically females, children, or those who are emotionally unstable. New users are easy to spot; they don't know the chat room lingo or have entered sites such as "Newbie Chats" or the "Getting Started Tour." Stalkers will even go so far as hacking into their victim's Internet profiles to get more information on their chosen target.

Showing vulnerability is a red flag to a stalker. Talking about feeling depressed, upset, or abused in an open chat is a magnet for some predator to quickly pick up on. They usually start messaging you privately, offering words of comfort, trying to lure you into a false sense of security.

How Do You Know You're Being Cyberstalked?

Most cases of cyberstalking usually begin with either sexually harassing comments, a flame war (a back and forth argument that gets out of hand), or someone with an extremely technical background who tries to show off by harassing Internet users, busting into chat rooms—even networks. There is a distinction to make regarding this behavior: A cyber harasser is someone who commits these acts, but moves from victim to victim. The cyberstalker commits these acts, but keeps coming back to the same victim. Both are obnoxious, but the latter is more likely to turn dangerous.

Avoid Becoming a Victim of Cyberstalking

Following these tips can greatly reduce your risk of attracting a cyberstalker:

- **Never specify gender when registering for services online.** As with your mail and bills, use only your first initial and no title: C. Smith.
- **Never give out personal information through the Internet** unless you have thoroughly investigated the site you're providing it to through simplesimon.com or another reliable information Web site.
- **Do not use your real name** for your screen name or user ID.
- **Use a gender-neutral screen name** Yes, I know the name Safety Chick is not gender neutral, but it is for business, not personal use.
- **Don't share any personal information in online public spaces.**
- **Change your passwords often.** This can be a hassle, but better safe than sorry.
- **Do not sign or fill out guest books** that are found on various Web sites throughout the cyberworld.

"Chat" Safely

Follow these precautions to avoid hooking up with a cyberstalker in a chat room:

○ **Use secure chat rooms;** those that don't permit tracking of your ISP address.

○ **Never use your real name in a chat room.**

○ **Choose a chat room nickname that doesn't offend others.**

○ **Be extremely careful when sharing information about yourself online.**

○ **Never give out your work e-mail address for personal business.** Hackers can find out too much information about you that way: where you work, your real name.

○ **Avoid getting into arguments online, a.k.a. flame wars.** Stalkers or harassers love to pick an opposing view just to irritate others; don't fall for their childish behavior—stop arguing or leave the chat room.

○ **Remember, people who use the Internet are strangers.** Treat them as you would a stranger you meet on the street: courteous, yet careful.

○ **Get out of a conversation with someone online who has become hostile or sexual.** Log off or go to another chat room.

○ **Don't flirt online.** In the real world, flirting or making sexual advances toward someone you don't know or have never seen is risky; the cyberworld is no different.

Instant Messaging

Various e-mail providers offer an instant messaging service that allows members to talk to each other when they are online. This can be great fun—just ask my friends who constantly harassed me while I was trying to write this book—but it also can attract unwanted communication from outside your circle of friends. Strangers can gain access to e-mail addresses by looking through instant messaging directories that are listed by mail providers. Yahoo, America Online, and Microsoft Network all have directories. To avoid being listed in any of the directories, refer to your e-mail provider's security section to find out how to eliminate your name from their lists, and follow these precautionary measures:

○ **Sign up for mail anonymously.** Use an "anonymizer" service as discussed on page 129.

○ **Never use your real name.**

○ **Don't put any information in the "user profile" section.** If it is required, be extremely general.

○ **Do not accept messages from anyone who is not on your "friends" list.**

○ **Don't accept messages that are sent to multiple recipients.**

○ **Disable the "Web aware" feature.** No one needs to know when you are on- or offline.

○ **If you get messages from people you do not want to hear from, put them on the "ignore" list.**

"If you don't double-click me, I can't do anything."

—John Aniston, actor

What to Do if You Are Being Cyberstalked

These are a few recommendations if you find yourself a possible victim of harassment or stalking on the Internet:

○ **Save all evidence.**

○ **File a report with local law enforcement.**

○ **Report the incident to your ISP.** Contact the system administrator and find out about their abuse policy.

○ **Report the incident to the ISP of the harasser or stalker if you know it.**

○ **File a report with your appropriate ISP channel:**
Abuse@yahoo.com or postmaster@yahoo.com.
○ **Change your screen name.**
○ **Change your password.**

The laws against cyberstalking differ from state to state. Because of the newness of the Internet, cyberstalking, like stalking, is a relatively new subject to law enforcement. The laws against the crime of stalking have advanced quite a bit in the last ten years. If you are a victim of cyberstalking, check with local police to find out how the laws read in your state. For more direct help, contact a victims' advocate Web site, like www.wiredpatrol.org or www.wiredkids.org. They can assist you in filing a report and help you with any questions you might have.

SPAM—Not Just Meat in a Can

How to protect yourself from spam mail and virus plagues

Of course the subject of Internet safety and abuse lends itself to many fabulous Web sites. It has been impossible for me to wade through all this information and choose which ones to mention. Therefore, in the resource chapter, I will mention as many sites as possible that could prove useful. What I looked for were sites that gave information in layman's terms—easy for computer illiterates like me to understand. One site that I found extremely helpful was www.emailabuse.org. Run by Marshall Hays, this Web site is dedicated to informing Internet users of potential abuse and providing them with tools to avoid becoming a victim and to fight back. Much of the information in this section comes from emailabuse.org.

What Is E-mail Abuse?

E-mail abuse is characterized as the use of electronic mail to harass, annoy, or cause harm to the e-mail recipient. Abuse can take the form of threatening e-mail, or bulk mail with the intent to slow productivity or cause damage to the recipient's system. This is a worldwide problem; anyone with e-mail is at risk.

Many people link the term *spam* to this abuse. While spamming is quite annoying, not all spam mail is linked to criminal activity. For this chapter, I want to focus on the criminal or consumer fraud aspect, not the ethical debate that can ensue when talking about businesses' right to spam.

A Word about Spam

According to spamabuse.org, "the term *Spam* is to flood the Internet with many copies of the same message in an attempt to force the message on people who would not otherwise choose to receive it. Most spam is commercial advertising, often for dubious products: get-rich-quick schemes or quasi-legal services. Spam costs the senders very little—most of the costs are paid by the recipient or the carriers rather than the sender."

Spam with a Criminal Twist

Regardless of the ethics of spam mail, the criminal aspect arises when a spammer's sole purpose is to go information fishing. One of the first things my cyberguru John Flowers warned me about was the fraudulent side of spamming. There are deviants who set up a spamming business for the purpose of snagging valid e-mail addresses to gain access to your personal profile. After accumulating your personal information, these trollers then sell all the information to anyone who will pay for it—potentially including pedophiles, stalkers, or identity thieves.

Investigate Yourself

To find out what kind of personal information is already out there about you, search the Web yourself. Go to sites like switchboard.com or dogpile.com. They offer various types of searches on people for a fee, depending how in-depth you want to get.

Whatever You Do . . . Don't Click the Box

Most spam mail that you receive will have a "take me off your list" box for you to check. What is disguised as a courteous service is really a trap. One click in the box tells them you are a valid e-mail address and you'll get even more junk mail. According to Kaitlin Duck Sherwood, author of the *Overcome E-Mail Overload* series of guides, "If you have an ISP with millions of users, like America Online, and you have a user name made up of English words or a common name, spammers will guess it." So remember, don't click the box—hit DELETE instead.

Use a Filter to Sift through the Problem

An easy way to cut down on unwanted e-mails or unwanted solicitations is to set filters that come with your e-mail software. Refer to an anti-spam Web site to learn how to recognize characteristics that most spam mail contains, and set your filters accordingly. If you really want to get serious, there are more aggressive anti-spam products that you can buy. Programs like SpamEater or SpamBuster use artificial intelligence to figure out what's spam and what's not.

How to Trim Your Spam

According to emailabuse.com, there are several things you can do to avoid becoming a victim of e-mail abuse. So far, there are no foolproof measures, but following these suggestions can greatly reduce your risk.

○ **If you have any doubts as to the authenticity of the sender and/or the content, do not respond to it.** They may sell your address to every spammer out there. Instead, contact the service provider directly in hope of getting the offender's service terminated.

○ **Report Internet fraud to the Federal Trade Commission or the National Consumer Complaint Center.**

○ **Get a free e-mail account somewhere online specifically for newsgroups and when registering on Web sites.** Most spammers use programs to gather addresses from these sources. The spammers will get this address and all the junk e-mail will flood this mailbox instead of your working one.

> "To err is human, but to really foul things up requires a computer."
>
> —Farmer's Almanac, 1978

○ **Don't post your actual e-mail address on your Web site.** Again, spammers have programs that can scan your pages for your address.

○ **Use mail filters.** They are not always completely accurate, but they can cut back on the number of junk e-mails you receive.

Beware of Viruses

Another danger of opening unsolicited mail is the possibility being attacked by a virus. These can quickly destroy valuable data and leave devastating damage in their wake. What's more annoying than getting a virus from someone you know because they opened something they shouldn't have, which then infiltrated their address book and passed it on to you? There are software programs that you can install on your computer that protect you from most viruses. The most popular, Norton AntiVirus, works pretty well to keep out most viruses. But remember: Your anti-virus software is only as good as the frequency of your updates. Experts update their software every day. You can do this by programming your software to update your system frequently; for maximum protection this should be done daily.

How to Ward off Viruses

Most viruses are spread through ignorance. According to email abuse.org, the following can help prevent infection.

○ **Do not open attached files, especially .exe files, if you are not positive where they came from.** Virus developers use something called "social engineering" that can make a harmful attachment look like it came from your friend Jane, when, in fact, Jane unknowingly has the virus, and it sent itself to everyone in Jane's mailbox. Another "red flag" are attatchments that have two periods, like myfile.doc.scr; be suspicious if you see them. It's smart to verify with the sender what they sent before you open the attachment.

○ **Run virus scanning software or virus releases.** As stated above; Norton AntiVirus or other anti-virus product.

○ **Keep up with current news on virus releases.** If you know what's out there, you can take measures to avoid infection.

Taking steps to stop spamming or reporting e-mail abuse helps every Internet user. The more people who start reporting abuse or quit opening or buying products from spam advertising, the better chance honest users have of putting the bad guys out of business.

E-Commerce: Friend or Foe?

Protect yourself while shopping online, and how to spot a cyber scam

This section is based on the same concepts covered in chapter 5, A Girl's Gotta Shop, on identity theft and credit card fraud. Hopefully by now I have driven home the point that you should guard your personal information with your life, sharing it only with people that you know and trust. The same is true for the Internet. But while the idea of inputting your credit card number onto someone's e-commerce Web site might seem risky at this point, there are security measures you can take to ensure safe cyber shopping.

Wanna Buy a Watch?

Just as you wouldn't buy a Cartier watch—at least not a real one—from a guy on the street, you shouldn't buy anything from a site that you don't know. Before you make a purchase, check it out. Sites like mysimon.com or streetprices.com offer a service that will give you a report on the company you are thinking of patronizing. Mysimon.com will rate a company by product price and reliability. If the place that you are searching for is not listed or gets a bad rating—shop elsewhere.

Look for the Logo

Most reputable e-commerce sites carry a logo that ensures their standard of business. Verisign is one of the leaders in digital trust services. They manage e-commerce transactions with name services, authentication services, and payment services. When you see the Verisign logo on a Web site, you know that your transaction is being managed by a reputable source.

Learn to Spot Scam Sites

Learning to recognize banner ads, e-mails, and companies that are a scam is an important tool. Mortgage loans, sweepstake notices, and travel bargains are all candidates. Any offer that requires you to fill out personal information is not a good choice. Most banner ads and spam advertisements are from companies that have no business plan and use cheap forms of advertising to attract suckers.

> The most overlooked advantage to owning a computer is that if they foul up there's no law against whacking them around a little.
>
> —Joe Martin, cartoonist

The Toolbar Can Tell a Story

Referring back to David Nielsen's site, fightidentitytheft.com, "one key to identifying fraudulent sites is to look at the address toolbar in your browser. If it says anything other than the domain name of the site you think you're visiting (wellsfargo.com for example), it is probably a scam and you should report it to the company immediately. . . . Another variation is getting a message that states 'the credit card you used to sign up for service is invalid or expired and the information needs to be reentered to keep your account active.' If you ever get a message like this be very, very careful. It might be best to call the company, unless you are absolutely confident that it is a valid message."

To sum up the philosophy every cybergirl should adopt when using the Internet, I will quote from wiredpatrol.com: "The Internet is an amazing place. But the fact that it is a wonderful place to work, play and study does not mean users shouldn't be aware of its dark side. The Web mirrors the real world." The truth is, you are more susceptible to credit card fraud or identity theft every time you leave a credit slip at a restaurant or store than you are when shopping on a reputable Web site. Use your cyber Safety Chick common sense and you should be fine.

The SAFETY CHICK Checklist

SAFETY MEASURES TO FOLLOW WHEN SURFING THE NET

- ☑ Check your computer privacy settings—cookies, logon status.
- ☑ Install firewall protection.
- ☑ Remove all personal information/profiles from your ISP records.
- ☑ Do not use your real name for screen name, password, or instant message.
- ☑ Do not give out personal information in online public spaces such as chat rooms, bulletin boards, and guestbooks.
- ☑ Change your passwords frequently.
- ☑ Do not open or accept mail if you are not positive where it came from.
- ☑ Report e-mail abuse to the Federal Trade Commission or at any anti-abuse Web site.

Chapter 9

Keep Your Hands to Yourself!

Domestic Violence Is *Not* a Family Matter. . . . It's a Crime

One night, home from college for a visit, I was having dinner with my parents and my older brother. Though we were used to traffic sounds because our house was on the corner of a relatively busy street, we were startled to hear a young woman screaming. By the time my brother and I ran outside, the woman was being thrown out of a slow-moving pickup truck. Thankfully, she landed in the ivy along the road. When we got to her, she was huddled up in a ball, crying. My brother touched her shoulder and when she looked up, we were shocked to see that it was a childhood friend of mine, whom I knew quite well. She immediately blurted, "Don't call my parents . . . my Dad will kill him." Sadly, she continued this tumultuous relationship with her so-called boyfriend (some friend!), and she continued to get knocked around. Somehow, I just don't get the romance and excitement of being thrown from a moving vehicle.

Domestic violence is an epidemic in this country. Thankfully, the laws are starting to get really tough on offenders. As women, we need to take responsibility as well. Learning to recognize abusive behavior before you get in a situation that you can't get out of is a great place to start. Our country is a world leader in cutting-edge programs, shelters, and organizations for women who are victims of domestic violence. But in order to get help, you need to understand the definition of domestic violence and how to recognize signs or behavior so you do not become a victim.

Love Means Never Having to Say, "I'm Sorry I Punched You in the Eye"

And other lessons in recognizing domestic abuse

One of the best organizations in the area of domestic abuse education is the National Coalition Against Domestic Violence. (Look to the Resource Guide at the end of the book on how to reach them.) They have defined what battering is and the different forms it takes.

Domestic abuse is a way for a person to establish power or control over another person and can take many forms. It may include emotional abuse, economic abuse, sexual abuse, using children, threats, intimidation, and brute force. Women are the most common victims of this violence, but elder and children abuse is not uncommon. The batterer (or abuser) believes that he is entitled to control another. All of the following forms of domestic abuse are crimes.

Physical battering. The abuser's physical attacks or aggressive behavior can range from bruising to murder. It often begins with what is excused as trivial contacts, which escalate into more frequent and serious attacks.

Sexual abuse. Physical attack by the abuser often is accompanied by or culminates in sexual violence wherein the woman is forced to have sexual intercourse with her abuser or take part in unwanted sexual activity.

According to the American Medical Association, between two and four million women every year are battered by their spouse or partner.

Psychological battering. The abuser's psychological or mental violence can include constant verbal abuse, harassment, excessive possessiveness, isolating the woman from friends and family, deprivation of physical and economic resources, and destruction of personal property.

The most important thing to remember about battering is: It escalates. It often starts with behavior like name calling, violence in the victim's presence (like punching a fist through a wall in anger), and/or damaging objects or pets. It may escalate to restraining, pushing, slapping, and/or pinching. The batterer also might throw a punch, kick, bite, or trip. Sexual assault and throwing the victim around might come into play as well. Finally, the behavior may become life-threatening—choking, breaking bones, or using weapons.

Red Flags

There are certain telltale signs or conditions that might indicate a mate's propensity for violence.

1. **Did he grow up in a violent family?** People who have been abused as children or in homes where one parent beats another have grown up learning that violence is normal behavior.

2. **Does he tend to use force or violence to solve his problems?** A guy who gets into fights, likes to talk tough and has a quick temper is likely to act that way toward his wife and kids. Does he punch or throw things when he gets upset? Does he overreact to problems or frustration? Is he violent toward animals? Does he have a criminal record? (That one is an obvious beacon of warning.) Any or all of these behaviors may be signs of a person who resolves dissatisfaction or aggravation with violence.

3. **Does he abuse alcohol or other drugs?** There is a strong link between violence and problems with drugs and alcohol. If he refuses to admit or accept that he has a drug dependency or alcohol problem and refuses to get help, *do not* think you can change him.

4. **Does he have strong traditional ideas about what a man should be and what a woman should be?** Look, this isn't the 1950s anymore; marriage is a partnership, not a dictatorship. Does he think a woman should stay at home, take care of her husband, and follow all his orders and directions? Does he prohibit expression of ideas or concerns? Do you feel like a prisoner in your own home? This mindset leads to dysfunction and destruction.

5. **Is he jealous of your other relationships?** Not just other men that you may know, but also with your women friends and family? Does he keep tabs on you? Does he want to know where you are at all times? Does he not let you socialize with your friends without him coming along? Does he isolate you at his side constantly? *Remember: Possessiveness leads to aggressiveness.*

6. **Does he have access to guns, knives, or other lethal instruments?** Does he threaten to use weapons against people to get even? Does he have a fascination with guns or other types of weapons? (A guy with a healthy fascination with cars or sports is a better bet.)

7. **Does he expect you to follow his orders or read his mind?** Does he become unusually angry if you do not fulfill his every wish or if you cannot anticipate his every want and need? You are not Barbara Eden in *I Dream of Jeannie.*

> "Never be bullied into silence. Never allow yourself to be made a victim. Accept no one's definition of your life; define yourself."
>
> —Harvey Fierstein

8. **Does he go through extreme highs and lows?** This behavior can make it seem as if he's two different people: really sweet and kind at one time and extremely cruel or violent at another.

9. **When he gets angry, do you fear him?** Do you find that you feel as if you are walking on eggshells around him? Do you always do what he wants you to do rather than what you want to do? Does a major part of your life revolve around not making him angry?

10. **Does he treat you roughly?** Is he physical with you if you do not do what he wants? Does he lash out at you if he is frustrated? Shoving, pushing, or kicking is considered rough treatment.

If the guy you're involved with has any or all of these traits, reconsider the relationship before it goes any further. *It's up to you to set standards for yourself.* While the wild, bad boy might be attractive and sexy in Hollywood movies, in the real world they lead to nothing but trouble and heartache. Set higher expectations for your relationships and you'll be surprised at the number of nice guys you'll attract.

R-e-s-p-e-c-t, Find Out What It Means to Me

Why and how to gain the strength to get out of an abusive relationship

If you are in an abusive relationship, you need to get the heck out. Life is too short to live with someone who treats you badly. It might seem too scary and overwhelming to contemplate leaving, but for the safety of yourself and your children, you need to do it.

You might be asking yourself, "Why does he treat me like this? I know deep down inside he loves me." According to the National Coalition Against Domestic Violence (NCADV), there are many speculations on why men batter their mates. They include: family dysfunction, inadequate communication skills, provocation by women, stress, chemical dependency, lack of spirituality, and economic hardship. These might be reasons why men batter women, but they are not the root cause. Removing these factors does not end the violence. The batterer begins and continues the behavior because he believes that violence is an effective method for gaining and keeping control over another person. Plus, he usually does not suffer any adverse consequences as a result of his behavior.

Historically, domestic violence has not been treated as a "real" crime. The evidence is the lack of incarceration and financial penalties for people found guilty of abusing their partners. Also, the batterers rarely are ostracized in their communities, even if it is known that they beat their partners, so they have no guilt or sense of wrong doing.

Abuser's Profile

Batterers come from all different backgrounds and have different personalities, but they seem to share certain traits and behaviors.

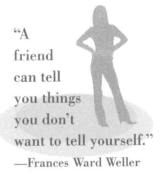

"A friend can tell you things you don't want to tell yourself." —Frances Ward Weller

Oink, oink: Batterers are basically male chauvinist pigs who do not see women as people, but as property or sexual objects. They do not respect women as a group.

Mr. Insecurity: Low self-esteem, a sense of powerlessness, and ineffectiveness in the world are their inner secrets. They may appear to be successful, but inside they feel inadequate.

It's all your fault: Batterers blame other people for their problems or behavior. Stress, something their partner did, alcohol, or other factors become the batterer's excuse for his violent reactions.

Leave It to Beaver: The batterer often is seen as charming and sweet by neighbors, but behind closed doors, it's another story. He can be calm and loving to his partner one minute and extremely volatile the next.

You belong to me: Character traits include extreme jealousy, possessiveness, and a bad temper. If a guy is unpredictable and/or verbally abusive, find another date.

Domestic violence happens in rich neighborhoods and poor neighborhoods. Batterers are of all skin colors and nationalities. Their behavior, characteristics, and personality profiles are what set them apart from other men.

Why Stay?

Why do women stay in abusive relationships? To many people, the thought of staying in a violent, demeaning situation is incomprehensible. It is difficult to understand what would prevent a victim from leaving. But for millions of women, the reasons are very clear:

"You can turn painful situations around through laughter. If you can find humor in anything, even poverty, you can survive it."
—Bill Cosby

He's got her by the purse strings. If a woman has at least one child and is not employed outside the home, all of the cash, property, and other assets are likely to be controlled by her spouse or partner. This makes it very difficult for a woman to move out and support herself and her child financially. For some women, it would mean a substantial drop in the standard of living for her and her child, and the guilt associated with that also prevents her from leaving.

Together forever. Many clergy and secular counselors are trained to encourage couples to stay together and "save the marriage," no matter what, rather than acknowledge the problem and assist somehow to stop the violence. Victims also may feel that divorce is not a viable solution. For the sake of the children, some abused mothers feel that a violent father is better than no father at all.

Nowhere to run, baby; nowhere to hide. Even a restraining order does little to protect the victim if the abuser chooses to return and repeat the assault. There has been an increased public awareness of domestic violence and a number of shelters have been opened to help keep some of these women safe. Unfortunately, there still are not enough shelters to support the needs of all victims of domestic abuse.

Failure is not an option. Many women are conditioned to believe that they are solely responsible for making their marriage work. If the marriage ends, they are failures. Women often are taught that their identity and self-worth are based on getting and keeping a man (no matter how badly he treats her).

All by myself. Some abused women become isolated from friends and family, either by the jealous, possessive partner or because they are trying to hide the signs of abuse from the outside world. In either case, these women feel isolated and believe they have no one to help them and nowhere to turn.

I'm dreamin'. The abuser rarely beats the woman all the time. During those nonviolent times, he may fulfill the woman's dream of romantic love. She believes that he's basically a good man with a bad temper. This reinforces her reason to stay. She also may rationalize that her abuser is basically good. When bad things happen, he just needs to let off a little steam.

Regardless of the reasons women stay in these violent, dangerous relationships, they need to get out. With education and strong support, more and more women are finding the strength to do so. There are many places that you can go for help. Programs like the Violence against Women Office through the Department of Justice, and the National Coalition Against Domestic Violence have wonderful support groups and services to assist you in your time of need. Just call their toll-free numbers or go to their Web sites for more information. Refer to the Resource Guide at the end of the book for more information and help near you.

Ready, Set, *Go*

How to plan your escape from a harmful situation and get to safety

It is extremely important for you to admit when you are in an abusive relationship. Be true to yourself and realize that there is a better world out there for you and your children, if you have them. If you don't, it's that much easier to get away.

If you are in a violent relationship, you'd better have a safety plan. The Dover, New Hampshire, Police Department, led by Chief Bill Fenniman, has one of the best safety protocols for victims of domestic abuse. The Dover PD's position on domestic violence is that aggressive prosecution of misdemeanor domestic violence cases ultimately will reduce homicides, spousal rapes, aggravated assaults, and related felonies. To that end, they have come up with a highly effective safety plan that all domestic violence victims should follow.

What You Can Do Prior to a Violent Incident

1. **Learn how to identify your spouse/partner's pattern of violence so that you can assess the potential danger to yourself and your children.** Most batterers have a trigger for their violence: when they are stressed out at work, if something has upset them, or if they have been drinking or abusing drugs. Be aware of what sets off your abuser and steer clear of him at these times.

2. **When possible, plan to leave before violence occurs and when your partner/spouse is not around.** Go to a safe place such as a domestic violence shelter or a friend's home. Make arrangements with a trusted friend, or a friend of a trusted friend whom your partner/spouse *does not know* to help you and your children. Ask them not to tell anyone that they are helping you.

3. **Notify a neighbor to be alert to strange noises or screams and to call the police when this happens.**

4. **If you can, get rid of all weapons in your home when your partner/spouse is nearing a violent stage or is in a violent stage of the cycle.**

5. **Teach your eldest or most responsible child to call the police and give your name and address if a violent incident is occurring and he or she is able to safely get to a phone.**

6. **Know your local battered women's shelter telephone number.**

7. **Plan where you will go in an emergency or dangerous situation:** a trusted friend's home, a shelter, or a safe family member's home.

"It's important that people should know what you stand for. It's equally important that they know what you won't stand for."

—Mary H. Waldrip

8. **If you believe your partner/spouse may come to the workplace, ask your employer not to talk with him.** Have the employer notify you if he shows up and wants to speak with you.

What You Can Do during a Violent Incident

1. **Leave the physical presence of the batterer, if possible.** Locate your escape bag (see page 155 for escape bag items) and leave the home or get to a room with a lock on the door and/or a telephone.

2. **Call the police 911 number, then call your local shelter for battered women.**

3. **Have your children call the police if you are unable to do so.**

4. **Scream so your neighbors can hear you; they may be more likely to call the police.**

5. **If you have to leave your children in the home, call the police immediately.**

6. **If you leave by car, lock your car doors immediately and drive to a safe place.**

7. **Check yourself and your children for injuries and go to the hospital or your doctor's office if necessary.**

8. **If you cannot get out of the violent situation, defend yourself to the best of your ability.** (Refer to chapter 10, Hand-to-Hand Combat.)

What Items You Will Need for Your Escape Bag

1. **Money.** Always keep some money set aside, if not in your own home, in a place where you have easy access, day or night. Plan to have enough money for weekend motel rent, telephone calls, gas, and food expenses for a few days.

2. **Keys.** Have two extra sets of your keys made for your car and your home; one for you to put in the bag and the other to give to a trusted friend.

3. **Extra clothing.** Have a bag with extra clothing for you and your children. Consider the fact that you may have to escape in winter or summer. Choose clothing that you can wear in either season.

4. **Important documents or papers.** Keep copies of all of the following in your bag:
   ○ **Social Security numbers (his, yours, your children's)**
   ○ **Birth certificates (yours and your children's)**
   ○ **Pay stubs (your husband's and your own)**
   ○ **Bank account numbers and checkbook**

○ **Insurance policies**

○ **Marriage license**

○ **Driver's license (yours and a copy of his)**

○ **Any legal papers related to property that you jointly own with your spouse/partner such as a car or house**

○ **Copies of your monthly bills**

○ **Valuable jewelry**

5. **Important telephone numbers:**

○ **Local police department**

○ **Local shelter**

○ **Victim assistance office**

○ **Probation officer**

○ **Your counselor**

○ **Defendant's counselor**

○ **Other: friends, children's school, etc.**

6. **Items of particular importance to you or your children.** For example, a favorite keepsake or special stuffed animal or toy.

Keep this bag in a place that is hidden from your abuser, but easy to get to—maybe somewhere on the front porch or hidden in the garage or kitchen. Don't leave it where he could easily find it and question what you are up to. If you have neighbors who are trustworthy, consider leaving the bag at their house. This action plan might seem like a lot to cover, but take things one step at a time, and you should be able to put the bag together in a few days.

Domestic violence is a complicated issue. When children are involved, it's even more heartbreaking and difficult. Talk to your local shelter or victim assistance office to get more information on how to manage your personal situation. Remember: There is always a way to get out of an abusive relationship. Be strong, have courage, and use the common sense of the domestic violence shelters and law enforcement agencies that are there to help you. We Safety Chicks are behind you.

The SAFETY CHICK Checklist
DOMESTIC VIOLENCE ESCAPE BAG

- ☑ Money—enough for a few days of lodging, telephone calls, gas, and food
- ☑ Keys—extra set for your car and home
- ☑ Extra clothing—for you and your children
- ☑ Important documents/papers—birth certificates, Social Security numbers, pay stubs, bank accounts, insurance policies, marriage license, driver's license, property ownership papers, copies of monthly bills
- ☑ Important telephone numbers—police, shelter, victim assistance office, probation officer, counselor, other
- ☑ Items of personal importance—sentimental item, valuable jewelry, stuffed animal or toy for children

Chapter 10

Hand-to-Hand Combat

Should You Stay or Should You Go?

One of the greatest self-defense stories I've ever heard was told to me by one of the loveliest women I have ever met. I was doing another one of those "Women who fought back and won" talk shows. I met her in the Green Room; that's show biz talk for the waiting room. She was a charming woman in her late 50s, very refined, soft-spoken, and classically dressed. We chit-chatted about life and where we were from. All I knew about her story was that she had been attacked in her own home.

When we got onto the set, the host asked for particulars. The reserved woman I had met earlier suddenly transformed into this Rambo-like warrior, telling of that fateful night. She was asleep in her bed; her 80-year-old aunt was sleeping down the hall. She awoke to find a naked man crawling on top of her; he had broken in through the bedroom window. But this demure lady was not your everyday victim. Immediately, she grabbed the perpetrator's privates. I believe her words were something like, "I just dug my nails into his penis and scrotum. I kept twisting and twisting until he fell to the ground. I held on tight as I dragged him out of the house. Once we got to the front yard, he was screaming so loud, he woke the neighbors, and they called the police. When the paramedics came and examined him, they found several of my broken nails imbedded in his family jewels."

The story above demonstrates that sometimes you need to use physical force to get out of a dangerous situation. This chapter examines the philosophy of conflict resolution further, but also introduces self-defense moves and other deterrents that can aid you in your time of need.

The three tools you need to overcome your fear of being a victim are strength, courage, and common sense. You will need your strength to physically defend yourself against your attacker. You will need your courage when dealing with any threatening situation. And you will need common sense to assess your attacker and the situation you are faced with, if and when it comes to that. Once you have put all these things together, your chance of surviving an attack is strong.

Hold That Thought

How to get out of a potentially violent situation before it's too late

Of course, the most important tool to use when assessing a threatening situation is your intuition. Use your antennae to tell if someone is following you. If you are walking down a sidewalk, use the reflection of a storefront window to track a potential attacker. If you are in a car, make a turn and then another to see if someone is following you. Using your intuition allows you to avert a potentially threatening situation before it happens. The key is to *avoid* a potentially violent setting by being aware and removing yourself from harm's way. If you find yourself face to face with a predator, there are several things you can do to avert danger and possibly save your life.

The first thing to do is to understand who you are dealing with. Much of the information on this subject that I share in this chapter comes from the philosophy of Matt Thomas, the creator of the highly acclaimed self-defense program Model Mugging. Matt combines psychological empowerment with simple but devastating defense moves. Model Mugging is the most efficient self-defense philosophy that I have ever come across. Matt has a gift of turning an extremely physical and emotional process into commonsense empowerment to which all women can relate. He has written a book called *Defend Yourself!: Every Woman's Guide to Safeguarding Her Life,* which is thorough and excellent. Here is an excerpt which provides a great example of how wisdom can overcome fear:

Cowards in the Dark

An imaginary enemy is often more frightening than an actual one. When we are children, our greatest fears are often of monsters. As we get older, we may encounter children, sometimes bigger than we are, who are bullies. Looking back with adult eyes, we know those monsters were not real and that the bullies were themselves afraid and insecure and, in most cases, would have been cowards had we stood up to them.

The average rapist is not a huge monster but instead averages five feet eight inches tall and weighs one hundred and fifty pounds.

The average rapist is not a brave and fearless conqueror. He's a coward. All rapists are cowards! Research shows that in half of all rape attempts, any resistance from the woman causes the rapist to run away. The completion rate of rape against a single, unarmed woman is 33 percent. By contrast, the completion rate against a woman armed with a club, knife or firearm is only 3 percent.

. . . Men who attack woman are, like people who make obscene phone calls, cowards in the dark, relying upon your fear. If you don't allow a man the power of intimidation, he may very likely run away to find a more cooperative victim.

Cowards, of course, can do great harm. But your fear of them is only useful if it propels you into meaningful action, and your best chance for that is if you respect the threat but also recognize your ability to stand up to it.

Animal, Vegetable, or Mineral?

Men who commit violent offenses against women are wild animals. Therefore, to be safe you need to understand how an animal thinks and behaves. Matt believes that in order to fully learn how to protect yourself against an attacker you must understand that the root of all attacks is based on the prey versus predator mentality. What does a tiger do when his prey runs from him? He runs after the victim at full speed. The same is true for an attacker. If you turn and run, he will run you down. So, unless you are an Olympic sprinter or you have a clear shot to safety, you need to learn how to turn and face your predator with clarity and confidence.

The Freeze Walk Stance

Self-defense begins with a fighting stance, one that is designed to potentially diffuse the situation without physical force and, at the same time, enables you to explode into decisive action. According to Matt, it is called the "freeze walk" because that is exactly how you learn it. You are walking. Suddenly your heart pounds—you've heard a sound, and your intuition kicks in. Someone calls you or someone is coming toward you. You feel that you are in danger. Stop and face the direction of the danger. Again, do not run unless you know where you're running and have absolute confidence that you can escape.

Before we get into the details of the freeze walk stance, here is an overview of how the movements should look:

1. Feet shoulder-width apart
2. One foot ahead of the other
3. Toes pointed forward
4. Knees slightly bent
5. Weight on the balls of your feet
6. Pelvis tucked under
7. Arms at your sides, then swing up, crossing your arms in front of your face in a half-circle motion. Finish with your elbows pointing down in front and close together
8. Hands up at eye level, protecting the face, waving across each other; palms out, fingers spread
9. Arms bent, armpit at 45-degree angle

There are many more defense and moves scenarios to learn about if you're interested. Because this is not solely a self-defense book, I am not able to cover them all. The moves in this chapter give you a really good foundation, but again I recommend taking a self-defense class like Model Mugging to train appropriately. For more information on Model Mugging, look to the Resource Guide at the end of the book.

Stop, Look, Assess

Whenever you are approached in a manner that you perceive as threatening, scan the area to assess the danger. There is always the possibility that your attacker is not alone. When you are in an adrenaline state, you can get tunnel vision, and you might not see another attacker until it is too late. It is imperative that you use your peripheral vision as you take your stand. Force yourself to turn your head left and right to see exactly who you are dealing with.

Wax On, Wax Off

As you quickly bend your elbows and discreetly swing your forearms and hands in front of your face in a half-circle, you must say "No," in a low, serious growl. Done right, this move can appear to the attacker that you are not offering a challenge but that you are acknowledging and respecting his potential power. It tells him that he has nothing to prove. You aren't communicating, "Back off, Creep;" but rather, "Stop, you are making me uncomfortable and invading my space." You have now set a boundary that tells your attacker not to approach.

The two advantages of the freeze walk stance from a self-defense perspective are:

1. You have the opportunity to take the attacker by surprise because you have given him no sign of resistance.
2. Because he anticipates no fight, he will probable try to grab you, therefore making it easier for you to defend.

Put On a Show

The next step is to show your threat display. Think of an alley cat when it approached by an unfamiliar feline: back arched and tail fluffed, usually making a growl or some sound of warning. Body language is everything. You must speak to your attacker's "inner core," which is animalistic. You do not want to appear threatening, but you also don't want to appear weak. Be calm and firm and in control.

Two Little Letters—Big, Big Word

There are many reasons as to how and why saying the word "No" can be the difference between life and death.

1. Forcefully yelling the word "No" in a low, guttural voice throws your attacker off guard.

2. Using a loud, threatening growl instead of a helpless whimper or scream sends a message to your predator; think of an animal when it fights, the one that growls wins, the one that whimpers loses.

3. Exhaling the word "No" replaces the natural inhale of fear with the exhale breath of anger.

4. The word "No" said in a stern manner is a command to stop behavior that all mothers direct at their children. This might trigger the criminal's subconscious and throw him off.

5. A loud growl attracts attention; a loud scream frightens people. Onlookers have a tendency to stop to watch a fight; therefore, someone might stop to help. If you scream, people might be frightened and run away.

In addition to a threat display and establishing boundaries, you also need to give the attacker an option to de-escalate. This is a statement that should be made after you have said, "No."

Talk 'Em Down
Using a phrase like, "Leave me alone, I don't want any trouble," in a commanding growl gives the assailant a chance to back off. Do not say, "I'm going to kick your ass!" No matter how tempted you might be, these words excite an attacker, and could be his invitation to fight.

Sticks and Stones
One of the most intimidating weapons an attacker can use is words. Vile, scary words said in an abusive and threatening way are terrifying, if you allow them to be. Remember, "sticks and stones can break your bones but names will never hurt you." Focus on his actions, not on his words. Say to yourself, "Come on, buddy, is that the best you can do?" or "Yeah, well, your mother wears army boots."

No Fisticuffs

Make sure that your hands are not making a fist; this sends a signal to the predator to use fists back. Hands in front of your face with fingers spread allows you to be in the "ready" position without signaling to your attacker you are set to punch.

According to Matt Thomas, 750 women who took the Model Mugging course reported attempted attacks against them by predators after taking the class. Of those, 550 were able to thwart their potential attackers just by using the voice and stance of a threat display. Remember, a predator is nothing more than an animal. Anything that you can do to shake up his pattern gives you a chance to escape and avert an attack.

> If a shark is hit while going after potential prey, or if anything happens to alter the pattern of their attack, they usually retreat and regroup. Rarely do sharks make a second attempt toward the same prey.

Putting It All together

The combination of these three actions—threat display, establishing boundaries, and giving an option to de-escalate—is your freeze walk stance. These moves should be performed all together in a fluid motion.

1. Stop, turn and assess the situation. (Turn your head to the left and right to properly scan the area.)
2. Get into a firm stance: feet shoulder-width apart, one foot slightly in front of the other, hips square.
3. As you forcefully say the word "No," your arms smoothly swing up in front of your face, fingers spread, hands slightly waving, elbows as close together as you can get them.

4. Follow up with, "Leave me alone, I don't want any trouble."

You have now set the stage for what happens next. It is now up to your attacker to lead you into your next move.

Man Your Battle Stations

Time to tap your strength, courage, and common sense

You've given your attacker all the chances to abort and he's made the wrong decision. It is now time to make the transition to combat. In the next section, I will teach you three moves that you can use in various combinations to defend yourself effectively. But first I want you to understand how to pick your battleground and utilize your surroundings. If you're in front of a plate glass window, move away. If you're on stairs, move up or down. The key is to remove yourself from an area that your attacker could use against you and to take control.

Obstacle Course

If a predator is making his way toward you, put a physical obstacle between you and him. For example, get on the other side of a parked car, lamppost, magazine rack—anything that makes him work to get you. This throws him off balance. If he has to come between two parked cars, take that opportunity to step to the side of one of the cars, wait for him to step between the two and then let him have it. If you can jump behind a thorny bush or hedge, go for it. Predators don't like to work too hard for their prey. Make it tough; wear him down. If you are on a sidewalk, make him step off the curb and hit him when he's midstep. Stairs are tricky because you don't want to be thrown down them. If you have a chance to make him step up or step down, however, do it. Remember, getting your attacker off balance is the key. Use your surroundings to your advantage.

A Night at the Improv

Improvised weapons are a great addition to your self-defense moves. They can be found just about anywhere and are quite effective against a predator. Matt has classified these into three categories: projectile weapons, club-type weapons, and cutting weapons.

Projectile weapons are things that can be thrown into your assailant's eyes that can temporarily blind him or cause him to lift his head, enabling you to do a "heel palm strike" to the nose (see page 172). Common things to throw are sand, dirt, coins, or hot coffee.

Club-type weapons are objects that you can use to jab or hit your attacker. Aim for the head; usually your attacker will grab the object. Take that opportunity to go for his privates, one of the most vulnerable areas for men. Common objects to strike with can be a purse, umbrella (club and jab), briefcase, or backpack. Think Ruth Buzzy: the little old lady on the old comedy show *Laugh-In* who used to beat the dirty old man over the head with her purse.

If your object has a sharp end, like an umbrella or pen, jab at the eye or neck. A model in New York once fended off an attacker by beating him about the face and head with the heel of her Ferragamo pumps and her Chanel purse.

If someone is wielding a knife or sharp object at you, wrap a jacket or sweater around your hand and forearm to fend of the attack. Swing your arm in a figure-eight motion.

—Matt Thomas

Cutting weapons are implements such as nail files, broken glass, or bottles. The best place to use these weapons on your attacker is in his eyes, face, or neck. However, Matt says that these will not stop the attack cold. Knife wounds rarely incapacitate a person. In fact, many people don't realize they've been stabbed for minutes after an attack.

Improvised weapons are to be used against your attacker as a distraction to enable you to make your move. For example—a handful of dirt or sand thrown in the eyes, even a fistful of loose change can hurt. Any of these will be a deterrent to the predator, but probably not a disabler. You must be ready to use your self-defense moves to do the rest.

Model Behavior

Moves to use against your attacker

The following information was taken from Matt's book *Defend Yourself!* and what I learned from taking the course. Practice these moves at home, in front of a mirror. Once you have them down, invite a friend over or ask your boyfriend or husband to role-play with you. Think of it as a rehearsal for a play. You don't want to try these moves for the first time when your life depends on it, just like you wouldn't take your driver's license test without test-driving a car first.

Practice Makes Perfect

When you are in a life-threatening situation and you must defend yourself, rational thinking goes out the window and is replaced with subconscious reflex. Therefore, the following self-defense skills, practiced correctly and sufficiently, will take over.

1. **Don't freeze up.** All humans have the natural tendency to freeze in a frightening situation. Remember when you were a kid and heard a noise in the middle of the night and you froze like a statue under your sheets? Many believe this comes from our ancestors, who were once the prey of larger animals. Most predators that stalked them detected movement better than shape, so holding completely still became a means of survival. And yet, when the predator is another human being and you're not hiding, it doesn't do you much good. It doesn't make any sense to freeze, but instinct can be a powerful thing.

2. **Don't stop breathing.** Breathing patterns alter under stressful conditions. Anger, for example, can cause a person to forget to breathe in, or to breathe more rapidly. Fear can cause a person to forget to breathe out. Any of these disruptions of breathing during physical combat can make you winded and sap your energy when you need it the most.

3. **Don't bite your tongue or lip.** This is a common nervous response to danger or fear. Even though Michael Jordan is famous for sticking his tongue out when slam dunking—not to mention some of his other jaw-dropping moves—it's best to keep your teeth away from your tongue and lip. The force of your own punch can cause you to bite down, which is painful and might cause a distraction you cannot afford.

The solution to these three problems is one word: "No." Shout it each time you strike with your hand, your elbow, your lower thigh, or your foot. Try shouting "No" when you are holding your breath or biting your tongue or lip. You can't. Fiercely shouting the word "No" is empowering and propels you into action.

Where to Hit

Before you learn how to hit, you need to know where to hit. Chances are, your attacker will be bigger and stronger than you. To compensate for that, you must hit him where he is most vulnerable. According to Matt, there are two key targets: the groin and the nose.

Hit Below the Belt

No matter how big and strong a man is, he can be incapacitated by a forceful blow to the genitals. Use the front of your thigh, not your knee. Do not aim for the front of the body. Instead, thrust your thigh up and under the groin. The idea is to crush the testicles up into their pelvic bone. (Ouch!)

Be Nosey

The other highly vulnerable part of a man's body is the nose. Push gently on your own nose and see how much it hurts. Just a little bonk can cause your eyes to water or shut. A forceful strike to the nose can cause blurred vision, bleeding, dizziness, a broken bone, even unconsciousness. Even if you miss the nose, a blow to the face or head will do some damage.

The One-Two Punch

Because the two target points are at different parts of his body, he cannot defend both areas at once. So, the idea is not to knock him out with one punch, but rather, keep the pummeling going until he is unconscious or gets the hell away from you.

If he covers his groin, go for the nose; when he guards his face, go for his testicles. Strike whichever is most accessible. If he's grabbing for your arms, you've still got your legs. If he grabs your legs, you've still got your arms. You become a lean, mean fighting machine before he knows what hit him.

How to Hit

Now that you know why to hit, who to hit, and where to hit, you need to know how to hit. From the threat display stance—one foot slightly in front of the other, hips square—your first defensive strike is at the upper target, the nose. Matt calls this potentially powerful punch the heel palm strike. He teaches this punch for several reasons, primarily because it is very easy to learn. (Mastering the correct way of performing a fist-punch so as not to break the knuckle or wrist can take years.) But the positioning of the heel palm strike also allows you to keep your hands up in a protective position. So, if you miss the blow, you can still protect yourself against your attacker.

Palm Power

If you put enough power behind the base of your palm, you can break any man's nose. From your threat display stance, a heel palm strike is an easy and natural move. If your right foot is back, lead with your right palm. If your left foot is back, lead with your left palm. The move is sudden and explosive. The striking arm extends while the same hip thrusts and slightly twists forward; most of the power comes from below the waist. All momentum and power should be focused on the attacker's nose. Don't forget to yell "No" with every strike. Your other hand stays up, elbow bent, protecting the face.

Do not fully extend the arm during the move—it can give you a hyper-extended elbow, which is bad for your tennis game, among other things. Jab forward until the elbow is only slightly bent, then pull back to the protective hands-up position. Keeping the elbows in and parallel with your shoulders allows you to deliver a powerful offensive strike. In addition, when thrusting your palm forward, you also can deflect an oncoming inside jab to your face. When bringing your arm back to the guard position, you can deflect an outside jab to the side of your head. Now you're groovin'.

Push 'Em Back, Shove 'Em Back, Waaay Back

One of the objectives of the heel palm strike is to knock your attacker backward, away from you. When you strike his nose, imagine your hand driving into his skull. Matt thinks a good way to practice is to kneel on a mat or firm mattress and alternate the right and left strike in repetitions of three. Don't forget to yell "No" with each strike. (Make sure to tell family members that you are practicing your moves.) Concentrate on the heel of the palm striking the surface with force. Shake your body out after every repetition.

Thunder Thighs

The heel palm strike will draw the attacker's attention to his head. When it does, he will expose his other target area for you to pummel. Your next move is the thigh to groin move. Like the heel palm strike, this move is sudden and explosive. Use the thigh of the leg that is back and drive it forward, up, under, and through his groin with the portion of the thigh bone closest to your knee. Shout "No," then step forward. Make sure to keep your hands up because this move will put you right next to your attacker.

Get a Little Closer

As uncomfortable as this may sound, the closer you are to your assailant, the better. Your urge will be to push away, but doing so allows the attacker to get the advantage. Staying in close and using your heel palm strike to the nose and thigh to the groin and head gives you a fighting chance.

Perfecting the Move

Done correctly, the thigh to groin move can lift your assailant off the ground, crushing the testicle to the pelvic bone—quite a problem for him if your attacker is trying to commit sexual assault. Even if you miss the groin, a strike to the thigh, hip, or abdomen creates pain and/or distraction which will cause him to expose his other target: the nose and head. Practice the thigh to groin move in slow motion, three times with each leg.

Stay A"Head" of the Game

If the attacker isn't lying on his back or side by now, then he will, as any man will tell you, bend forward to hold his groin, leaving his head unguarded. Keep moving forward and drive the other thigh into his head and shout, "No." There isn't a specific target on the head; anywhere is fine—you don't want to rely on fine motor skills when you are in an adrenaline state. Aim for the center of the head, but a solid blow to any part of the head can knock him out. As with the thigh to the groin move, the thigh to the head is a thrust forward with the entire body that should drive your thigh up at his head. Think of driving a football through the uprights for an extra point with your thigh.

Practice the thigh to the groin move followed by the thigh to the head. It's like a high step with one leg and then a high step with the other. Then practice all three moves together. Heel palm strike to the nose, high step forward with same side leg, thigh to groin move, then high step forward with other leg, thigh to the head. With each move yell the word, "No."

"Common sense and a sense of humor are the same thing, moving at different speeds. A sense of humor is just common sense, dancing."

—William James

From the Top

Matt recommends practicing each move and technique individually in order to get a fair amount of precision. But he feels that in order to make these moves become second nature, you must practice the entire sequence together. It is helpful to do the moves in front of a mirror at first. Be aware of your body position. Make sure you follow all the detailed instructions of the freeze walk stance. Are your feet shoulder-width apart, knees slightly bent? How about your elbows, are they tucked in close to your body? How does your body position feel? Are you standing firm and solid? If someone walked by and shoved you, could they easily push you over? If so, make sure one foot is slightly in front of the other for balance. Ready? Set? Go . . .

1. Scan the situation
2. Freeze walk stance
3. Heel palm to the nose while shouting "No"
4. Thigh to the groin while shouting "No"
5. Thigh to the head while shouting "No"

Practice these moves in sequences of three, then rest before doing another three. Keep in mind that these moves are a response to a very specific kind of attack—frontal and standing by an unarmed assailant. However, the concept of the freeze walk stance combined with the high/low target area strike provides the basis for all other defense moves. Mastering this sequence of moves should give you confidence and defensive flexibility in virtually any situation.

Remember that every situation is different. There is no way to prepare for exactly what might happen if you are ever approached by an attacker. The key is to become extremely comfortable with the three moves. Then, if attacked, just keep repeating the moves until your assailant retreats or falls to the ground.

We (Might) All Fall Down

If your attacker is able to push you to the ground or you accidentally fall, be prepared. Practice falling backwards from the standing position, using a gymnastics-type mat or mattress. With your hands in the ready position, cross one foot in back of the other, bend your knees and gently fall down. Be sure to keep your hands up, and let your legs and rear end absorb the fall. Use your stomach muscles to keep your torso upright and quickly roll onto your side. Many a wrist has been broken by putting an arm out to absorb a fall. Falling hurts, but falling the right way allows you to continue defending yourself without incurring serious injury.

I Get a Kick Out of You

Once you hit the ground, roll to your side. If you are on your right side, get up on your right forearm, not your elbow, with your left hand touching the ground for balance. Immediately start kicking with the leg on top. Slightly bend the bottom leg and use the top leg as you would your arm. Think of the heel palm strike, but with the heel and bottom of your foot. Aim for the head and the groin. If your attacker bends over to try to attack, kick his head. As he falls back from the kick, aim for the groin.

Use your arms and butt to pivot around as your attacker moves. A good visual is that your arms and butt and bottom leg are on a lazy susan and your top leg is a powerful piston pumping into your chest and out, forcefully kicking your target points. Done right, when performing the kick your chest will almost be touching the ground as your rotate your hips forward and propel your flexed foot and leg toward the target. This is called the side thrust kick, but think of it more as a side/back kick.

Bootylicious

This is where having a power booty really pays off. All of your kicking power is derived from the gluteus maximus muscles. Focus and tap into that large muscle group. Bring the knee into your chest and drive your foot out with all your Bootylicious strength—a term of endearment made immortal by the songstress chicks Destiny's Child. Get into position and practice this kick in slow motion. Focus on your target, looking over your shoulder. In your mind, aim for the head and groin areas. Practice three times on each leg. Make sure to follow through with the leg.

Always practice your defense moves with complete follow-through. Stopping short of your target or drawing back your leg before full extension is a bad habit to get into. Remember: When you are in an adrenaline state, you do what you have practiced. Pulling back before you hit your target isn't going to do you much good in the heat of battle.

Like Riding a Bike

If you end up on the ground and can't get to the side, use a front thrust kick. To get the power for this kick you must be up on your forearms and rear end. Think of peddling a bicycle in the air. It is a one-two combination. Aim for the head and groin; one foot high, one foot low (don't forget to yell, "No" with every kick.) This kick doesn't have as much power as the side thrust kick, but it does have the advantage of fast repetitions and easier accuracy. Remember, your attacker can't protect both areas at the same time, so look for the target opening and keep going for it. Picture yourself playing the game at the carnival where you smack the gopher with a wooden mallet when he pops out of his hole. The mallets are your powerful legs, and the holes are the unprotected target areas of your gopher—I mean, assailant.

Give 'Em the Ax, the Ax, the Ax
(For All of My Stanford Friends)

The last effective kick is called the ax kick. This kick should be used when your attacker is down but not unconscious, or if he is getting up to try to attack you again. This move is simple and is done in the same position as the side thrust kick. Bring your top knee in toward your chest, but this time bring your leg up and swing your flexed foot down on his head or groin like an ax. The leg should remain slightly bent through the whole kick. Practice this three times on each side on your bed or mat, yelling "No" with each repetition.

"Karate is a form of martial arts in which people who have had years and years of training can, using only their hands and feet, make some of the worst movies in the history of the world."

—Dave Barry

It's Combo Time

Now, practice falling. Get used to using your legs and rear end instead of your arms to break your fall. Quickly roll to the side and practice your side thrust kicks, transition right into the front kicks and finish with the ax kick. Repeat three times on each side. To really get comfortable, practice various combinations in any order. There is no exact science to self-defense. The more ways you practice, the more situations you're prepared for.

Rising from the Ashes

Finally your attacker has stopped moving. He is either tired or unconscious or faking it. Proceed with caution. Carefully swing your legs around and stand up. Be aware of your surroundings. Walk toward your attacker with your hands in the ready position. Step above his head, but out of his reach and yell, "No." Quickly assess your situation. Is he getting up? Is someone else coming toward you? Are they friend or foe? If your attacker is getting up, begin using the defense moves again. If he is unconscious, find someone to call 911 for you.

Take a deep breath; try to calm down and realize that your mind and body just went through an extremely emotional and powerful event. Focus on the positive: You were incredibly strong, you had tremendous courage, and you used your inner wisdom—definitely a self-defense Safety Chick.

The SAFETY CHICK Checklist
SELF-DEFENSE SEQUENCE

☑ Scan the situation—be aware of your surroundings

☑ Freeze walk stance—threat display, establish boundaries, option to de-escalate

☑ Heel palm strike—heel palm to the nose while shouting "No"

☑ Thigh to groin move—upper thigh thrusts up and under groin while shouting "No"

☑ Thigh to head move—second thigh thrust into attacker's head while shouting "No"

☑ Assess—make sure assailant is unconscious or incapacitated

☑ Get help—ask someone to call 911

Chapter 11

Pick Your Poison

Self-Defense Products to Help You Stay Safe and Feel Empowered

In college, one of my sorority sisters was riding her bike back to the dorms after playing tennis. A man jumped out from behind one of the buildings and grabbed her bike. She quickly grabbed her tennis racket from her basket and began swinging. She smacked the guy on the side of the head, which knocked some sense into him, and he ran away. Her quick thinking and creative use of her tennis racket demonstrates that any object can be a weapon.

This story illustrates how quick thinking can be a lifesaver. As covered in chapter 10, Hand-to-Hand Combat, sometimes improvised weapons are a necessity. It does, however, pay to be prepared. Owning some type of weapon ensures your ability to defend yourself against an attacker or home invader. The key is to be extremely comfortable using whatever defense product you own.

You should think of self-defense products in two categories: one, to be used as a deterrent; and two, to be used as a debilitator.

For example, pepper spray is a deterrent. Sprayed in an attacker's eyes, it allows you time to remove yourself from harm's way. A gun, however, is a debilitator. If a bullet hits your attacker, chances are he will be severely injured or killed. Only you can determine which products are best suited for your situation. In order to decide, you need to examine the different options that are available.

Peter Piper Picked a Pepper

Pepper sprays, pepper foams, and other self-defense aerosols

Before you choose to carry a pepper spray or foam, realize that there are certain conditions when these products might not be the right choice. For example, if you are in an enclosed area, spraying your attacker with pepper spray can mean that you are also spraying yourself. If you are using an aerosol, rain or wind can affect where the spray ends up. However, defense sprays are still among the easiest and most effective protection products you can use.

Defense Spray 101

Self-defense sprays are made of irritating and inflammatory agents that can include combinations of tear gas, hot cayenne peppers, and ultraviolet dye. Sprayed in an assailant's face, it can cause extreme pain; it also causes the eyes to water and can make breathing difficult. The spray can reach anywhere from 8 to 20 feet, depending on the model, and can incapacitate an assailant for anywhere from 20 to 90 minutes, although if he is on alcohol or drugs of any kind, he might not feel the pain and be able to keep functioning.

OC/DC
Oleoresin capsicum (OC), more commonly known as pepper spray, is a derivative of hot cayenne peppers. Pepper spray's potency is measured according to Scoville heat units, or SHUs, named after the pharmacologist who discovered the valuable properties of the peppers, William Scoville. It is not the amount of pepper in a spray that makes it effective, but rather the SHUs. Most sprays contain 10 to 15 percent OC formula and about 1.5 to 2 million SHU.

OC is an inflammatory. This, unlike an irritant, causes the membranes to drain and swell; the eyes uncontrollably water or tear, and it inhibits breathing. All of these reactions are involuntary, and the substance is extremely effective whether your assailant is under the influence or not.

X Marks the Spot
One of the newest additions to defense sprays is ultraviolet dye. Sprayed on clothing or skin, the dye shows up under a black light. Law enforcement personnel and victims alike find this vindicating when the perpetrator is caught and feigns innocence. Once the black light shines on him, the situation becomes ultra-clear.

Spray or Foam
The difference between pepper spray and pepper foam is simple. One shoots like a spray of kitchen cleaner, the other dispenses in a stream of foam. The pepper spray is easy to use because it covers a larger area, so if you miss the eyes but spray around the head or face, the aerosol will still do its job. The drawback is lack

of effectiveness in wind, rain, or an enclosed area. The foam is a better choice, as long as you shoot it directly into the attacker's face.

Dispensing Choices

There are a couple of choices among pepper dispensers. One style is called the **forced-cone**. This forcefully sprays fine drops of the pepper solution in a mist that covers a distance of 8 to 12 feet. Another is the **broken** or **heavy stream**, which delivers a forceful and heavy blast of pepper. The can empties faster with this type of spray, but it is especially effective if you are in using it in a tight area, such as through a car window or other hard-to-reach area. The **fogger** is good for multiple attackers; the blast is like a small fire extinguisher and can render attackers incapacitated for at least 30 minutes. One drawback is the excess blow-back that can contaminate you in the process. The blow-back might cause you to tear and cough, but the direct hit will incapacitate your attacker for a good 30 minutes. The last dispensing choice is **foam**. As discussed above, this is the Safety Chick's favorite because it has virtually no blow-back spray and when sprayed in the face, saturates your attacker immediately. It's like carrying a can of shaving cream that packs a powerful pepper punch. Once the foam hits, it sticks and expands. Usually the perpetrator will try to rub it off, which smears the potent pepper solution all over his face. Foam is also effective in strong weather conditions and enclosed areas.

Take-Down Time

Several factors can determine how fast your attacker will be affected by the defense spray. Drugs or alcohol in the recipient's system can slow down the impact. Most normal take-down times are within seconds. In some instances, however, it can take a bit longer, so be prepared. Make sure you are a safe distance away from the attacker before you spray, so that you are not contaminated as well.

Legal Issues

Defense spray use is restricted in some states. For example, in New York you can purchase these sprays only through a licensed firearms dealer or pharmacist. In Massachusetts, you must purchase defense sprays though licensed firearms dealers. In Michigan, you can carry no stronger than a 2-percent concentrate of pepper spray. Cayenne spray is the only type of tear gas accepted and can be no larger that 35 grams per can. No combination sprays of tear gas and pepper spray is allowed. In Wisconsin, no tear gas of any kind is allowed; you can carry only pepper spray and it can be no stronger than 10-percent concentrate. It must be a 15- to 60-gram size and must have a safety lock feature. The best thing to do to ensure your legal safety is to check with the authorities on defense spray policies. It is up to you to find out exactly where and when it is legal to carry and use pepper or any other type of spray.

Try a Little

It is always a good idea to learn how to use defense sprays from a trained professional. Practice shooting the different types of sprays and see which one you like the best. In a controlled environment, you might want to try getting the spray in your eyes as well. That way if you are accidentally contaminated during the heat of battle, you will know what it feels like and will be able to function sufficiently to get out of a dangerous situation. The Safety Chick recommends doing this *only* under controlled conditions with trained professionals standing by.

During a TV show I did for Fox, they actually shot a guy with pepper spray right in the face. Now, granted, he was prepared to be sprayed, his body was ready for it, and a paramedic was standing by. The effects of the pepper were excessive tearing and burning of the eyes, coughing, and general discomfort. He did say that he could still function, but not as forcefully and deliberately as before the spray. After the show, he flushed his eyes for several minutes with water and took in a little oxygen. When he left the set a half-hour later, he was still not back to normal.

Cool Packaging!
The cool thing about defense sprays is that they come in James Bond–ish dispensers. For example, there's the pepper pen—it looks like a ballpoint pen, but when the cap comes off, look out. The pepper pager looks just like a business pager with a hidden nozzle on the side. The pepper lipstick case gives the phrase "Hot Lips" a whole new meaning (a Safety Chick favorite).

I want to reiterate that defense sprays are to be used as deterrents, to detain your attacker long enough for you to get away from him. Because of the ease of use, this is the most popular form of defense product sold.

Stunning

Stun guns, Air Tasers, and other electrifying products

If you think you might need a more forceful defense weapon, you can try a stun gun or Air Tasers. These incapacitate your attacker more severely and for longer periods of time but are less lethal than a gun.

Security Planet Corporation has one of the largest selections of self-protection products on the Web. They thoroughly describe every item and how they work. (Look to the Resource Guide on page 203 to learn more about Security Planet.) It is through their Web site and others that I researched these products.

There are two types of energy weapons: stun weapons and electro-muscular disruption (EMD) weapons.

Stun Guns

Stun weapons deliver shocks generally in the 7- to 14-watt range that interrupt the body's signals to the nervous system, which makes a person unable to physically function. (Only a small percentage of people can tolerate such electrical stimulation and fight through it.) The voltage does no permanent damage but can immobilize your attacker for several minutes. Even if the attacker is touching you, the current will not pass into your body.

This is how stun guns work: The voltage blast tells muscles to work at a rapid pace, which converts blood sugar to lactic acid. If you have ever exercised too much one day and tried to get out of bed the next, you know the feeling of lactic acid overload. That is a mild example, however. A one-second, 600,000-volt charge can stop an attacker in his tracks, causing him to drop to the ground with intense muscle spasms, feeling dazed and confused for up to 15 minutes. A five-second charge can leave him feeling like he fell from a two-story building and landed on the street.

Types of Stun Devices

Static charge guns. This gun uses an electrical charge with static to disrupt localized muscle groups. The electric charge can be anywhere from 9 to 24 watts at 100,000 to 600,000 volts, depending on the strength you choose. A 100,000-volt stun gun takes a 9-volt battery; a 200,000- to 500,000-volt stun gun uses two 9-volt batteries; and a 600,000-volt stun gun uses four 9-volt batteries.

The Muscle Man static charge gun. A special static charge delivery system allows this gun to give a "feels-like" shock of approximately 100,000 more volts than its rating. In other words, a 300,000-volt gun delivers a shock that is equivalent to 400,000 volts because of the phase-induction electrical delivery system.

Pulse Watt Myotron®. The shock from this device intercepts and neutralizes brain waves from the motor cortex part of the brain, affecting voluntary muscle control and aggression stemming from the hypothalamus. The pulse-watt works in $\frac{1}{1000}$th of a second, which causes the attacker to collapse, lose bladder control, and be completely immobilized for up to 30 minutes. It operates with 28 to 30 electrical watts and 25,000 to 32,000 signal-scrambling pulse watts.

Stun baton. Mostly used by law enforcement, this weapon is a nightstick or billyclub with a stunning effect.

The Drawback

One drawback of the stun guns is that you have to be touching your assailant for the shock to work. They are also somewhat bulky, so pulling one out and using it discreetly is a bit of a problem. You also must hold it against the person's skin for at least three seconds, which may not sound like much, but trust me, it's an eternity when someone is attacking you. The best places to have them ready for use would be in your home or car. Always check with a law enforcement professional to find out if stun devices are legal in your area.

Air Tasers

EMD weapons deliver a stronger 18- to 26-watt signal that overrides the central nervous system and directly affects neuromuscular control. Regardless of a person's pain tolerance or mental focus, these weapons will physically debilitate anyone. The most common type of EMD weapon is known as an Advanced Air Taser. It fires like a gun, but two canisters of compressed nitrogen fire two hook-like probes or "talons" on wires 15 feet long at a speed of approximately 135 feet per second. These talons attach to clothing or skin and deliver an electrical jolt that causes an attacker to lose the ability to perform any coordinated action.

Gives a Lickin' and Keeps On Tickin'

The most fabulous thing about the Air Taser is that after you have struck and incapacitated your target, the electric current continues to work with a preset time sequence. You can shoot the

"The only disability in life is a bad attitude."

—Scott Hamilton

Taser, drop it, and get to safety, all while the would-be attacker is still being zapped with the debilitating current.

I once demonstrated shooting an Air Taser on a television show. They set up a mannequin and I showed the host how easy the Taser was to load and shoot. In order to get the "perfect shot" for the show, I had to load and shoot the Taser over and over again. I was amazed at how easy it was and how quickly and effectively the probes hooked onto the mannequin every time. We even tried putting a heavy leather jacket on the mannequin, and the hooks latched on immediately; the current has the strength to penetrate through two inches of clothing.

FYIs about Tasers

○ If you miss your target and the attacker is still approaching, the Taser also can be used like a stun gun. Just touch the gun to the target's body and shoot.

○ The best way to use the Taser is to shoot your target while standing a couple of feet away. The talons work best when they are about 16 inches apart to receive the best t-wave flow.

○ While the Taser will leave your attacker dazed and confused for several minutes, it has no lasting aftereffects on muscles, nerves, or other body functions.

Legal Guidelines

Once again it is up to you to check with law enforcement about restrictions or laws pertaining to owning a stun device. States where it is currently illegal to own stun devices: Hawaii, Massachusetts, Michigan, New Jersey, New York, Rhode Island, Wisconsin, and District of Columbia. Even though a state might have no restrictions, cities within that state might. In Chicago, Baltimore, Philadelphia, and New York City it is illegal to carry a stun device. Even states that allow stun devices may have some sort of restrictions attached. For example, in Connecticut you must have a written permit issued and signed by the mayor, chief of police, or other security personnel. That is why it is imperative that you check with local authorities before you purchase any type of self-defense weapon.

The Drawback

Although I found the Air Taser easy to shoot, I was just shooting at a still target. Some law enforcement professionals have said that the wires and talons are somewhat hard to aim and sometimes miss their target. Make sure you are trained by a professional and become comfortable using the device. Practice and rehearsal help immensely if and when you find it necessary to use your weapon.

To Fire, or Not to Fire

Exploring the reasons to own a gun

Many people have asked me if I carry a gun. While I fully believe in the right to bear arms, to this date I do not own a gun. I have been trained to shoot guns, and I have learned about gun safety, but for me, personally, it is still an overwhelming responsibility. And yet writing this chapter has forced me to really think about owning a firearm.

One woman who has made a huge, positive impression on me regarding the use and ownership of guns is Paxton Quigley—definitely one strong-armed Safety Chick. Paxton holds seminars all over the country to teach women about firearm usage, safety, and training. She also has been a pioneer of woman empowerment and self-defense. Her best-selling book, *Armed and Female*, is a great read whether you own a gun or not. In it, she helps to clarify the various political positions on gun control and gives valuable information on the vast number of firearm choices.

Before I get into Paxton's philosophy, though, I have a few questions for you gun owners, and some advice.

1. **Do you have children?** If you do, keep your gun in a place where they can't get to it and make sure the safety is "on" at all times.

2. **Are you comfortable handling your gun?** Do you practice shooting it on a regular basis?

3. **Do you have a license to carry a gun?** Laws differ in every state, but in most states you cannot carry a gun on your person without a permit to carry a concealed weapon. The penalties are quite severe if you do not have the proper license.

When the "man" who stalked me came into my home and held me hostage, a gun could not have helped me unless I had it in my pocket. He surprised me in the hallway, holding a knife. If my gun were locked in the closet, do you think I could have said, "Hold on a second—I'm just going to go and grab my gun"? Another factor that a lot of people don't realize is that when you are in a life-threatening situation, your body shakes so hard it feels like you're going to explode. Your adrenaline makes it very hard to hold the gun straight, let alone aim at a target and shoot.

"I don't have time every day to put on makeup. I need that time to clean my rifle."
—Henriette Mantel

The stalker also had a concealed gun in his jacket pocket, so if I did not hit him with the first shot, who knows what would have happened? Even policemen have said to me that it is very difficult to use their gun in extremely tense situations—and they have been extensively trained to do so. There are thousands of women in the United States who are comfortable handling firearms. You just have to make sure that you are going to be one of them *before* you get your gun.

The Kid Factor

If you have children, you might want to think long and hard about owning a gun. The fact is, it's virtually impossible to guarantee that your child will never find or play with your firearm. There are several safety devices that you can put on your gun to make it difficult for a child to use—gun locks, pressure devices that go into the barrel, even trigger locks that prevent a gun from firing. You can also put your weapon in a combination or key lock box and put it in a safe hiding place away from your kids.

But, one of the best ways to prevent a firearm accident is to educate your children on gun safety.

Boys Will Be Boys

Law enforcement statistics show that boys between the ages of 10 and 19 are the most likely to be involved in gun accidents. As a mother of three boys, I can attest to their unrelenting curiosity and occasional lack of common sense. Take the time to educate your children on the dangers of guns. There are several instructional courses offered at shooting ranges or by other firearm professionals. Look to the Resource Guide at the end of the book for more information.

The Four Most Important Firearm Safety Rules to Teach Your Kids

1. **Never point a gun at anyone or anything.**
2. **Always assume that any gun you come across is loaded.**
3. **If you see or hear about another child who has a gun in his possession, notify an adult immediately.** Use caution when dealing with this type of situation; you do not want to provoke the child into using the gun against you. Calmly and discreetly remove yourself from the setting and get help.
4. **If you are visiting someone's house and you see a gun of any kind, leave the house immediately (remember to be discreet) and inform your parents.**

Be at Home on the Range

Ultimately it will be your decision whether to have a gun in the house or not, but realizing the potential for tragedy should be a major factor in your decision.

In her book, Paxton Quigley spells out clearly the demands of owning a gun:

> Having a gun for self-defense brings with it the responsibility of knowing how to use and maintain it. Without that knowledge, the firearm defeats your purpose and would not be relied upon to furnish protection. If you don't have the time or will to make time for instruction in the use of a self-defense gun, and if you cannot assume the responsibility of maintaining your skills with regular practice, it is my opinion that you should not buy a gun.

But she is also very clear about why a woman might want to own a gun:

> If for whatever reason, you think it is time for you to do your share to end the victim status of women, and if you can bear to undertake the attendant responsibilities, you should know that finding a gun in the hand of a potential victim is one of the most feared and avoided incidents a felon can imagine—feared and avoided even more than the police.

Paxton recommends that before you buy your gun, you should go to a target range and try out different models to see which one is best for you.

Firearms 101

Here is a beginner's glossary of firearm terms, types of guns, and their ease of use. Again, for more in-depth information, I refer you to Paxton's book *Armed and Female* or to a reputable firearms dealer.

Bullet. The tip of the cartridge that is loaded into the gun. The entire cartridge contains the bullet tip, gunpowder, a sparking device known as a primer that ignites the gunpowder, which causes the pressure that shoots the entire bullet down and out the barrel of the gun.

Caliber. This refers to the diameter of the bullet. It is measured by decimals of an inch. For example, a .45-caliber handgun shoots a bullet that is 0.45 inches in diameter.

Revolver. Considered the simplest of all handguns, this firearm works just as it sounds. The gun mechanically rotates a cylinder that brings a bullet cartridge up in front of the firing pin. The cylinder holds six or seven bullets, depending on the model, which means you only have six or seven shots. There are several different makes and models of revolvers. The simplicity of use makes it quite popular among women, but the disadvantage comes when reloading the revolver. Loading the gun one bullet at a time can put you at a disadvantage in your time of need, compared to other types of firearms.

Autoloader pistol (a.k.a. semi-automatic). This is an automatic *loading* pistol, but should not be confused with an automatic pistol, which *shoots* automatically. The cartridges stack on top of each other in a long narrow container called a clip or magazine. The trigger must be pulled every time you take a shot, but the used cartridge is ejected out of the top of the gun and the next cartridge feeds into the chamber ready to be fired.

There are single-action and double-action semi-automatic pistols. The concept behind the double-action is a safety feature so that owners can carry the gun with a cartridge in the chamber and the hammer down. The first pull on the trigger brings the hammer back; the following shots are then single-action.

One disadvantage of a semi-automatic gun is the strong jolt that occurs when the gun is fired. Many women find it hard to hold the gun steady and with enough pressure for the firing mechanism to work properly. As a result, this can cause the gun to malfunction.

Long guns. The rifle is considered one of the most lethal of all firearms. The hunting calibers were designed to shoot a bullet with great accuracy and distance. This is great if you are a hunter out in the woods looking for deer. It is not so great if you are in your home, using it for self-defense. The problem comes when the bullet passes through your attacker, through the wall behind him, and into the person sleeping in the other room. The shotgun also is known as a field rifle and was designed for hunting birds. One shotgun shell is filled with anywhere from eight large or 200 small pellets. There are different types of shotguns: autoloading, the pump shotgun, and a break-top model, which folds in half to load.

The main drawback in using a long rifle for self-defense is its size and maneuverability. Long guns are heavy and extremely hard to use in tight areas, not to mention almost impossible to conceal. Paxton and I agree—the long gun is purely a last resort when choosing a firearm.

Paxton Quigley's Four Guidelines for Selecting a Handgun

1. An autoloader or a revolver
2. A caliber that will suit your needs
3. A size of gun that you can handle comfortably
4. A grip that allows your finger to touch the trigger at the proper place

Once you have picked your handgun, you must make sure that you get the proper training in reloading, cleaning, marksmanship, and safety tactics for using your gun. There are many great training schools all over the country; check the Resource Guide on page 203 to find a program near you.

The Legal Side of Things

There are so many different gun laws in cities and states all over the country that it would be impossible for me to cover them all. You must check with local law enforcement on gun laws in your area. For laws and restrictions all over the country, refer to the National Rifle Association (NRA) or the Bureau of Alcohol, Tobacco and Firearms (ATF); again refer to the Resource Guide for more information.

Traveling with Your New Pal

I know that traveling with your gun can be difficult, but not impossible. If you plan on taking your gun in your car to a different state, check with their highway patrol on policies for transporting firearms. Many states require that you keep the weapon unloaded and in your trunk. Others let you carry a gun openly on the front seat or dashboard. No matter what the policy, you definitely want to be a law-abiding citizen wherever you travel, so you need to check local restrictions.

Flying High with Your Firearm

Federal law requires that when you fly, you must carry your firearm unloaded in locked luggage. Some airlines insist that any baggage containing a firearm be marked with a brightly colored tag, but this makes your luggage an easy mark for anyone wishing to steal a firearm. A better solution would be to bring another container, such as a lock box or briefcase, in which the firearm can be examined, marked, and enclosed. Then, put that container in your suitcase, which would remain unmarked. Again, check with airline security for exact rules and regulations.

Forget Foreign Lands

It is better to keep the firearms at home when traveling to a foreign country. Not many countries allow guns to be brought in. Paxton recommends that if you feel the need to have a gun in a foreign country, buy one there. When you're done, leave it at a local law enforcement office—don't even try to sell it.

Self-defense weapons can assist you in your time of need, but knowing how and when to use them takes strength, courage, and common sense. Be strong, brave, and smart always, Safety Chicks.

I want to end this chapter with a final thought from Paxton Quigley:

> It is apparent to me that the arming of American women needs to be brought out into the open, discussed and advanced—a rueful awakening, without a doubt, but perhaps the last frontier needed to be won by woman on the road to equality.

Afterword

You Go, Girl!

Taking Your Safety Chick Smarts to the Streets

Congratulations! At this point in your personal-safety education you're on your way to a secure future. Remember, don't feel like you need to incorporate all of these precautions right away. (As if!) With practice, they gradually will become as natural as brushing your teeth. In the meantime, use this book as a reference guide, one that you refer to and review throughout the different phases of your life. Reread the chapters that interest you most, and don't forget to share what you've learned with friends and family. (Or heck, buy them the book.) Every empowering conversation you have makes you a better Safety Chick.

I hope by now you've realized that personal safety involves so much more than crime prevention. Your bring-it-on attitude should cross over into every aspect of your life. Living with strength, courage, and common sense allows you to attain goals you never thought possible. But first, there's the little matter of fear to consider.

You can't hide from fear. In fact, it is completely normal to be afraid in some situations. Without your body's intuitive signals—the hair on the back of your neck standing up, the shortness of breath, the butterflies in your stomach—you might not realize you're in danger. But fear can also stand in your way. For many years I made a lot of stupid decisions based on fear. I moved out of Los Angeles, left my career, and moved home—I went into hiding. I regret those decisions to this day. The best way to deal with such debilitating fear is with knowledge. You need to identify and understand what you are afraid of and then learn more about it.

> "Courage is not the absence of fear, but rather the judgment that something else is more important than fear."
>
> —Ambrose Redmoon

For example, if you are afraid of being assaulted, focus on how to avoid becoming a target. Of course, you can start by rereading the relevant parts of this book and contacting a few of the organizations listed in the Resource Guide. But also consider taking your education one step further by enrolling in a self-defense class. Or, if you are concerned about your children being victimized on the Internet, take a course on computer safety at your local community college. If you think you need help getting in touch with your intuition, try a yoga class or meditation. Knowledge puts things in perspective. Just knowing that you can do something about your fear is instantly empowering.

After I was kidnapped I needed to face my stalker in court. The thought of standing four feet away from the man who had tried to harm me was unbearable. So, I started asking questions. I gradually learned how our legal system worked, what rights victims had, and what agencies there were to help me.

Understanding more about the court process made it less intimidating, and knowing there were supportive people by my side gave me confidence. Although it was still very difficult to be in the same room with the stalker, I didn't feel as helpless and vulnerable.

Whatever your fears are, the goal is to become proactive. Take charge of your personal safety, and you'll be amazed at how empowered you'll feel. Form a Chick Chat club with your friends. Share personal stories and tips, help one another implement safety procedures, and talk in detail about what you would do if you found yourself in a dangerous situation. Go to www.safetychick.com to learn more about Chick Chat clubs and to keep up with all the latest tips and resources for personal safety. Every shared tip is a positive step toward leading a savvy, Safety Chick lifestyle.

"To conquer fear is the beginning of wisdom."
—Bertrand Russell

Finally, since I'm such a clotheshorse, allow me to add a few Safety Chick accessories to your daily wardrobe.

Think of common sense as your shield. Despite conventional wisdom, courage doesn't have to come from within. Many of us women put the safety of our kids, our friends, or even our pets (weird, maybe, but true) above our own. Let that motivate you if you're ever threatened. Remind yourself that someone is relying on you to get out of the dangerous situation intact. For example, if some guy approaches you on the street, think to yourself, "Okay, jerk, I've got my kids and husband waiting at home for dinner. What the hell do *you* want?"

Think of wisdom as your helmet. As I said above, knowledge

is power. Knowing that you *can* do something if you get into a jam, and knowing *what* to do, helps you think clearly and focus to fight off or avoid trouble.

Think of strength as your sword. I believe that every woman should exercise and lift weights, not just because she wants to fit into that little black dress, but because she will *love* the feeling of the muscles in her body getting stronger. Working out gives a woman a natural toughness that obviously improves her ability to protect herself. It also increases her inner strength.

Living as a Safety Chick should be like wearing the perfect undergarment: It adjusts to the conditions at hand, keeps you tight in all the right places, and feels completely natural. Too bad it can't be had from the Victoria's Secret catalog!

A Resource Guide

Empower Yourself

Organizations That Can Assist You in Your Time of Need

Here is a list of organizations, arranged according to subject matter, that can educate you further or assist you if you need help. Many of these organizations have contributed to the information in this book. I thank them for that, and encourage you to take full advantage of their professional expertise.

Credit Card Fraud/Identity Theft

If you are a victim of fraud or identity theft contact:

Office of the Inspector General
U.S. Department of Justice—Fraud Report
Investigations Division
950 Pennsylvania Avenue, NW—Room 4706
Washington, D.C. 20530
Call: Hotline (800) 869-4499
Web address: www.usdoj.gov/criminal/fraud/Internet.htm

Identity Theft Clearinghouse
Federal Trade Commission
600 Pennsylvania Avenue, NW
Washington, D.C. 20580
Call: (877) ID-THEFT (488-4338)
Web address: www.ftc.gov

To find out information on shredding documents contact:

Shredit.com
Call: (800) 69-SHRED (74733)
Web address: www.shredit.com

Date Rape Drugs

For information on drugs contact:

Department of Justice
Drug Enforcement Administration (DEA)
Information Services Section (CPI)
2401 Jefferson Davis Highway
Alexandria, VA 22301
Call: DEA Intelligence Production Unit (202) 307-8726
Web address: www.dea.gov

The Drug Abuse Warning Network (DAWN)
Web address: www.samhsa.gov/oas/dawn.htm

For substance abuse help contact:

U.S. Department of Health and Human Services
National Clearinghouse for Alcohol and Drug Information

200 Independence Avenue, SW
Washington, D.C. 20201
Call: (877) 696-6795
Web address: www.health.org

Domestic Violence

If you are a victim of domestic violence contact:

National Coalition Against Domestic Violence (NCADV)
Violence Against Women Office (Diane Stuart, director)
810 7th Street, NW
Washington, D.C. 20531
Call: National DV Hotline (800) 799-SAFE (7233)
Web address: www.ncadv.org

Home Security

For information on finding a reputable locksmith or security
company in your area contact:

Your local police department (community affairs)
They will have a good idea of reputable alarm companies in your
town.

Securerite.com
They can direct you online to find a reputable locksmith/security
company.
Call: (800) 241-3930
Web address: www.securerite.com

Internet Crime

To file a report or learn more about Internet crime contact:

The Internet Fraud Complaint Center
A partnership of the FBI and National White Collar Crime Center
Web address: www1.ifccfbi.gov

Department of Justice
Computer Crime and Intellectual Properties Section
Call: (202) 514-1026
Web address: www.cybercrime.gov

Personal Safety Products/Weapons

To learn more about personal safety products contact:

Pepperspray.com
Encom Industries
P.O. Box 90245
Pasadena, CA 91109
Call: (800) 354-1019
Web address: www.pepperspray.com

SecurityPlanet.com
Security Planet Corporation
404 Terrace Hill Drive
Yakima, WA 98901
Call: (800) 981-9456
Web address: www.securityplanet.com

For information on firearms contact:

Paxton Quigley
Web address: www.paxtonquigley.com

The National Rifle Association
Web address: www.mynra.com

Rape

For help if you are a rape victim contact:

The Rape Abuse and Incest National Network (RAINN)
Call: (800) 656-HOPE (4673)
Web address: www.rainn.org

Rape Treatment Center
Santa Monica—UCLA Medical Center
1250 Sixteenth Street
Santa Monica, CA 90404
Web address: www.911rape.org

If you are a victim of Post-Traumatic Stress Disorder contact:

Post-Traumatic Stress Disorder Alliance (PTSDA)
Resource Center
Call: (877) 507-PTSD (7873)
Web address: www.ptsdalliance.org

Self-Defense

For information on Model Mugging contact:

Mark Vinci c/o Model Mugging
Web address: www.modelmugging.org

For more information on Matt Thomas:

Call: (818) 843-1848

Stalking

If you are a stalking victim contact:

National Center for Victims of Crime (NCVC)
2000 M Street, NW suite 480
Washington, D.C. 20036
Call: (800) FYI-CALL (211-7996)
Web address: www.ncvc.org

For questions concerning address confidentiality or other victim
services contact:

Office for Victim of Crime Resource Center
National Criminal Justice Reference Service
P.O. Box 6000
Rockville, MD 20849-6000
Call: (800) 627-6872
Web address: www.ncjrs.org

For questions regarding personal protection and threat assessment services in your area contact:

The Association of Threat Assessment Professionals
Web address: www.atap.cc

To find out about the anti-stalking law in your state contact:

Web address: www.findlaw.com

Travel Safety

For safety information concerning aviation contact:

The Federal Aviation Administration (FAA)
Aviation Safety Hotline, AYS-300
800 Independence Avenue
Washington, D.C. 20591
Call: FAA Safety Hotline: 800-255-1111
Web address: www.faa.gov

For security information concerning travel abroad contact:

U.S. Department of State
Bureau of Consular Affairs
Office of Public Affairs
2201 C Street, NW
Washington, D.C. 20520
Call: (202) 647-5225
Web address: http://travel.state.gov/travel_warnings.html

U.S. Customs Service—Headquarters
1300 Pensylvania Avenue, NW
Washington, D.C. 20229
Call: (202) 927-1000
Web address: www.customs.gov

Workplace Violence

To get more information on workplace violence contact:

The Occupational Safety and Health Administration (OSHA)
U.S. Department of Labor
200 Constitution Avenue
Washington, D.C. 20210
Call: (800) 321-OSHA (6742)
Web address: www.osha.gov

The National Institute for Occupational Safety and Health (NIOSHA)
4676 Columbia Parkway
Cincinnati, OH 45226-1998
Call: (800) 356-4672
Web address: www.cdc.gov/niosh/homepage.html

BRAVE Foundation
1228 8th Street Suite #104
West Des Moines, IA 50265
Call: (515) 453-8440
Web address: www.brave.org

Index

Underscored references indicate boxed text.

A

Acquaintance, stalking by, 91–92
Address confidentiality program, 107
Air Tasers, 188–90
Alarm systems, 61–67
Alcohol consumption, 46, 48, 148, 154
Answering machine, 58
Apartment safety, 54, 66
Association of Threat Assessment
    Professionals (ATAP), 89, 208
Automobile safety, 5–7, 24–26

B

Baton, stun, 188
Battering, 147. *See also* Domestic
    violence
Bills, paying online, 101
BlackIce PC Protection, 129–30
Body signals, recognizing, 7–9
BRAVE Foundation, 122, 210
Buddy system, 48–49
Burglary prevention. *See* Home security

C

Cameras, surveillance, 62, 65
Chat rooms, 131, 132, 134
Checks, personal information on, 101
Children
    domestic violence and, 146, 152, 157
    firearm safety, 191, 192–93
    Internet use by, 125–26, 130–32
    stalkers and, 98
Clothing, for travel, 32
Confidence, displaying, 32
Conflict resolution, 120–22
Co-worker, stalking by, 93

Credit bureaus, 80–83, 85
Credit cards, 16
    fraud, 9, 74–77
        information resources, 203–4
        reporting, 85
        protecting personal information, 101
        theft, 72–73
Credit report, 79–80
Cyberstalking, 94–95, 125, 133–35
    becoming a target, 132
    dealing with, 135–36
    locations of, 131

D

Date-rape drugs, 38–43, 204
DAWN (Drug Abuse Warning
    Network), 42, 204
DEA (Drug Enforcement
    Administration), 39, 41, 204
Deadbolts, 57
DMV (Department of Motor Vehicles),
    103–4
Dogs, home security and, 66
Domestic violence, 145–58, 158, 183
Doors, 56–58, 63
Drinks, drugging, 37–43, 48–49
Drugs, 37–44
    domestic violence and, 148, 150
    GHB, 40–41, 44, 49
    ketamine, 41–42
    MDMA, 38, 40
    Rohypnol, 38, 39–40, 44
    test for, 44

E

E-bills, 101
E-commerce, 141–43, 143